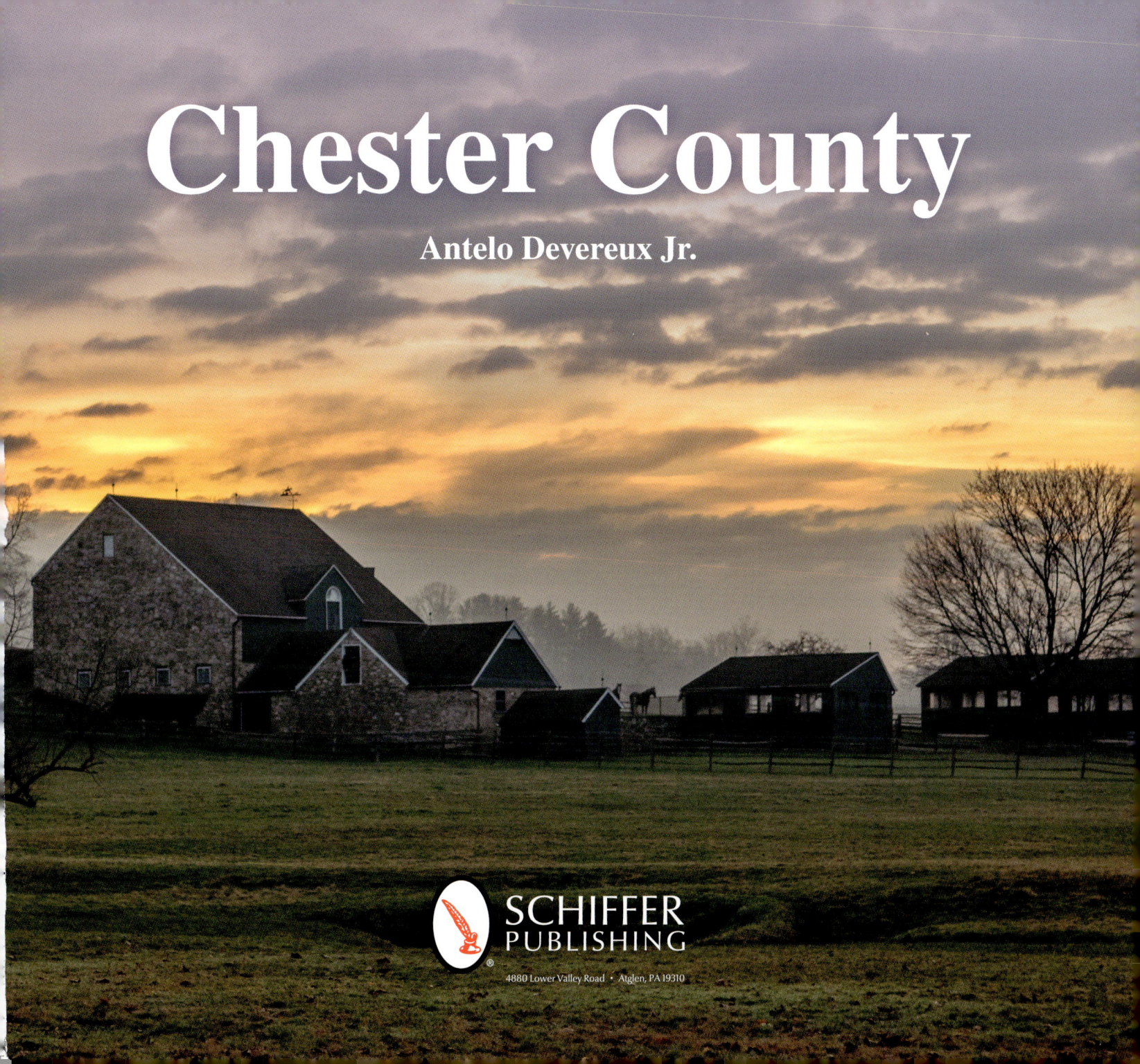
Chester County
Antelo Devereux Jr.

SCHIFFER PUBLISHING
4880 Lower Valley Road • Atglen, PA 19310

Other Schiffer Books by Antelo Devereux Jr.:
Brandywine Valley: A Keepsake, 978-0-7643-5574-5
Chester County Out and About, 978-0-7643-3625-6
The Jersey Shore: A Keepsake, 978-0-7643-5576-9
Eastern Shore Perspectives, 978-0-7643-4446-6

Copyright © 2021 by Antelo Devereux Jr.

Library of Congress Control Number: 2020943791

All rights reserved. No part of this work may be reproduced or used in any form or by any means—graphic, electronic, or mechanical, including photocopying or information storage and retrieval systems—without written permission from the publisher.

The scanning, uploading, and distribution of this book or any part thereof via the internet or any other means without the permission of the publisher is illegal and punishable by law. Please purchase only authorized editions and do not participate in or encourage the electronic piracy of copyrighted materials.

"Schiffer," "Schiffer Publishing, Ltd.," and the pen and inkwell logo are registered trademarks of Schiffer Publishing, Ltd.

Designed by Molly Shields

Type set in STIXGeneral/Cambria

ISBN: 978-0-7643-6155-5
Printed in China

Published by Schiffer Publishing, Ltd.
4880 Lower Valley Road
Atglen, PA 19310
Phone: (610) 593-1777; Fax: (610) 593-2002
E-mail: Info@schifferbooks.com
Web: www.schifferbooks.com

For our complete selection of fine books on this and related subjects, please visit our website at www.schifferbooks.com. You may also write for a free catalog.

Schiffer Publishing's titles are available at special discounts for bulk purchases for sales promotions or premiums. Special editions, including personalized covers, corporate imprints, and excerpts, can be created in large quantities for special needs. For more information, contact the publisher.

We are always looking for people to write books on new and related subjects. If you have an idea for a book, please contact us at proposals@schifferbooks.com.

and Dixon were enlisted to survey and establish the line that came to bear their names and forms the boundary between Pennsylvania and Maryland.

During the eighteenth century, Philadelphia and its surrounding area was the geographic, economic, and political center of the new country-to-be. The city was the largest English-speaking town other than London, and the Delaware River was the route to the outside world. Chester County's fertile land produced an abundance of food, and its streams and rivers provided energy for mills of all sorts. Rudimentary iron mines and furnaces provided forgings used during peacetime and wartime, especially in the northern part of the county. Remnants of those early years can be found scattered about the landscape.

With the influx of English, Welsh, and German settlers, growth radiated away from Philadelphia and the river. As a result, the county seat was moved west to a small community called Turk's Head, which then logically came to be called West Chester. The relocation of the political center happened with sufficient controversy that the portion of the county closer to the river was separated and became Delaware County in 1789. From then on, Chester County no longer had access to the river, nor did it share a border with Philadelphia, as do Bucks, Delaware, and Montgomery Counties. It became, as it were, one step removed from the city. In addition, the pattern of east-to-west movement and subdivision is quite apparent in the significant number of township names that start with "east" and "west."

Many of the immigrants to the region were Quakers who followed in William Penn's footsteps. They made a lasting imprint on the county—and indeed on the Philadelphia area—which is seeded with meetinghouses, a good portion of them still active. During the years preceding the Civil War, the county's Quakers and other families were an important part of the Underground Railroad, which harbored and guided slaves fleeing from the South. Not to be forgotten are the Mennonites and Amish, German and Swiss German settlers with Quaker ties. Language and religious and farming practices remain.

Today the natural character of Chester County is varied, with wooded hills and valleys in the north, and open fields and valleys in the south and west, all connected by streams and rivers. The man-made character of the county offers extremes of land uses—from dense suburban development on its eastern edge along the Schuylkill River to rural farms on its western edge along the Octoraro River. There are contrasts—high-rise buildings to log houses; shopping malls and general stores; high-speed, divided highways and dirt roads; speeding cars and Amish carriages. While agriculture, mills, and iron forging were part of the young nation's breadbasket and industrial base, steel and other manufacturing industries have declined and been replaced by high-technology companies. Agriculture continues to remain a major part of the economy, especially with the advent of mushroom farming. In addition, a significant portion of the county remains relatively undeveloped considering its proximity to Philadelphia—a result of successful and determined efforts to maintain open space and save land from development.

I hope the images herein will convey a sense of Chester County as I see it.

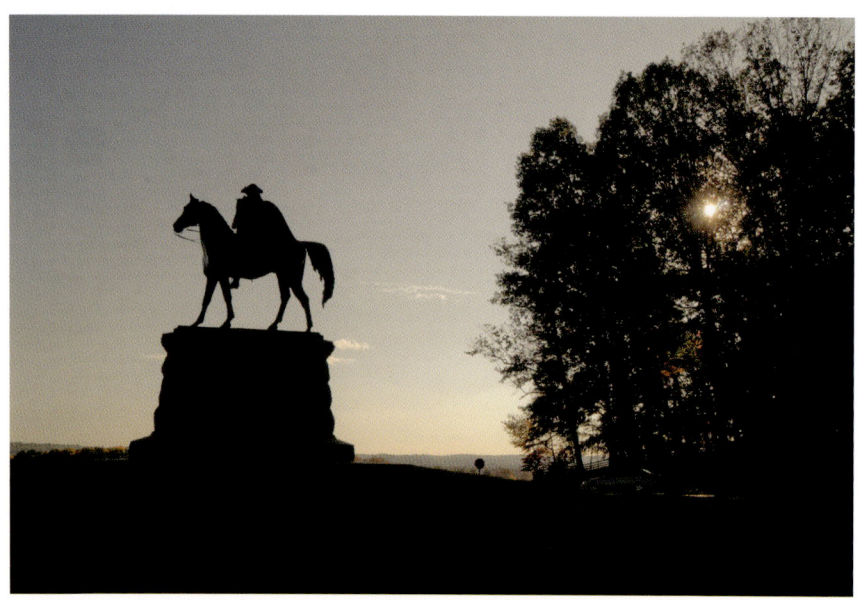

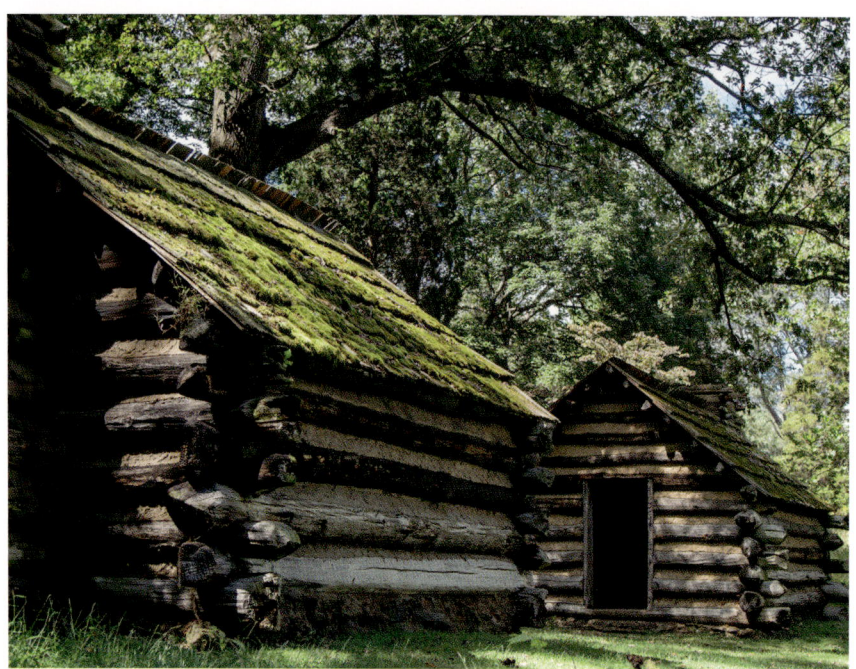

Valley Forge National Historic Park
A statue of Revolutionary War hero General Anthony Wayne looks toward Chester County, where he was born in nearby Waynesborough.

Valley Forge National Historic Park

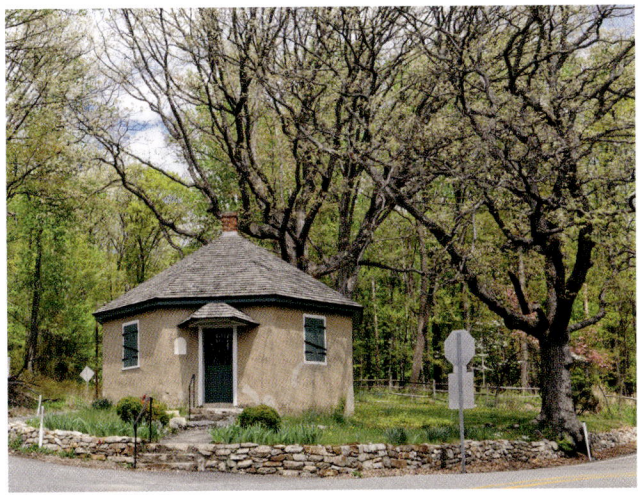

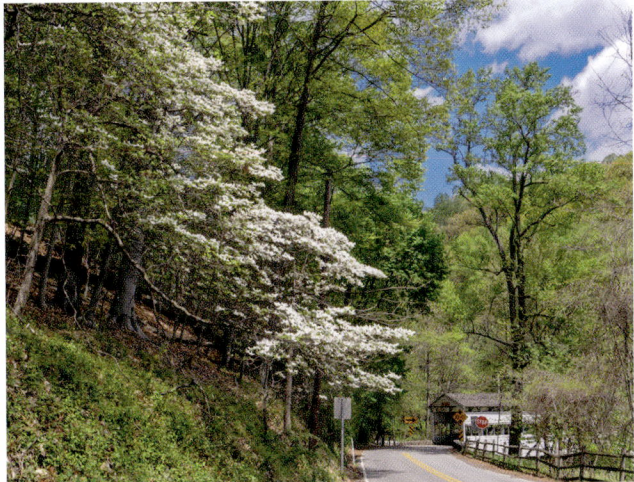

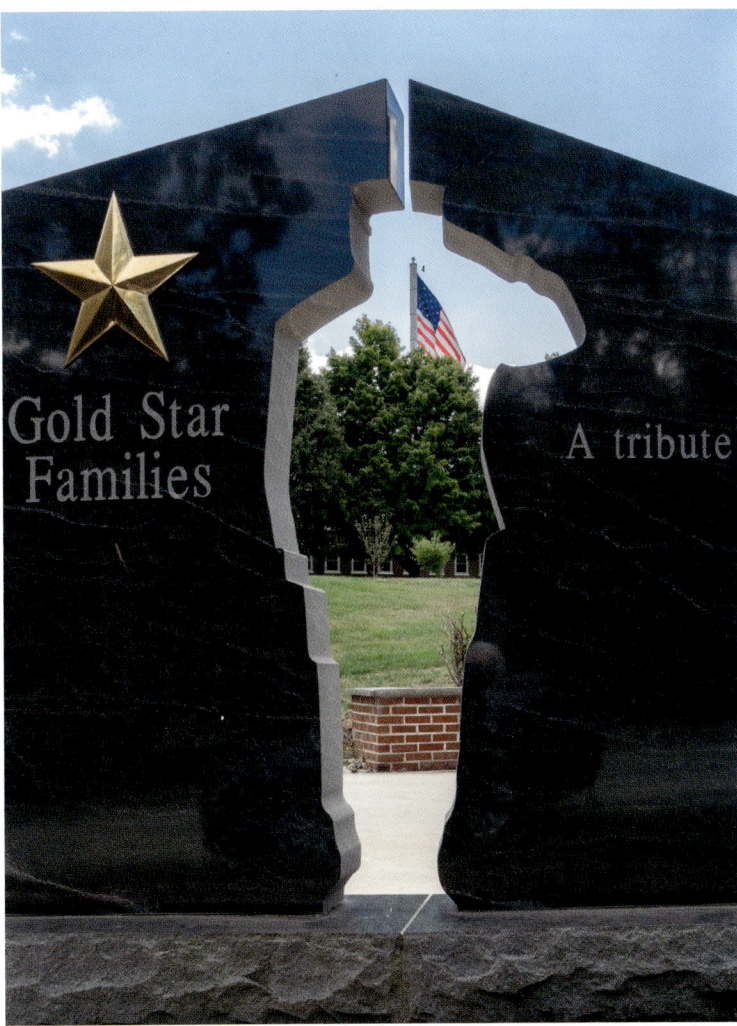

Tredyffrin Township
Diamond Rock School. The octagonal plan was a popular form of school construction in the early nineteenth century. Multiple grades could be taught individually and supervised collectively.

Valley Forge
Knox–Valley Forge Dam Covered Bridge

Valley Forge
Freedom Foundation

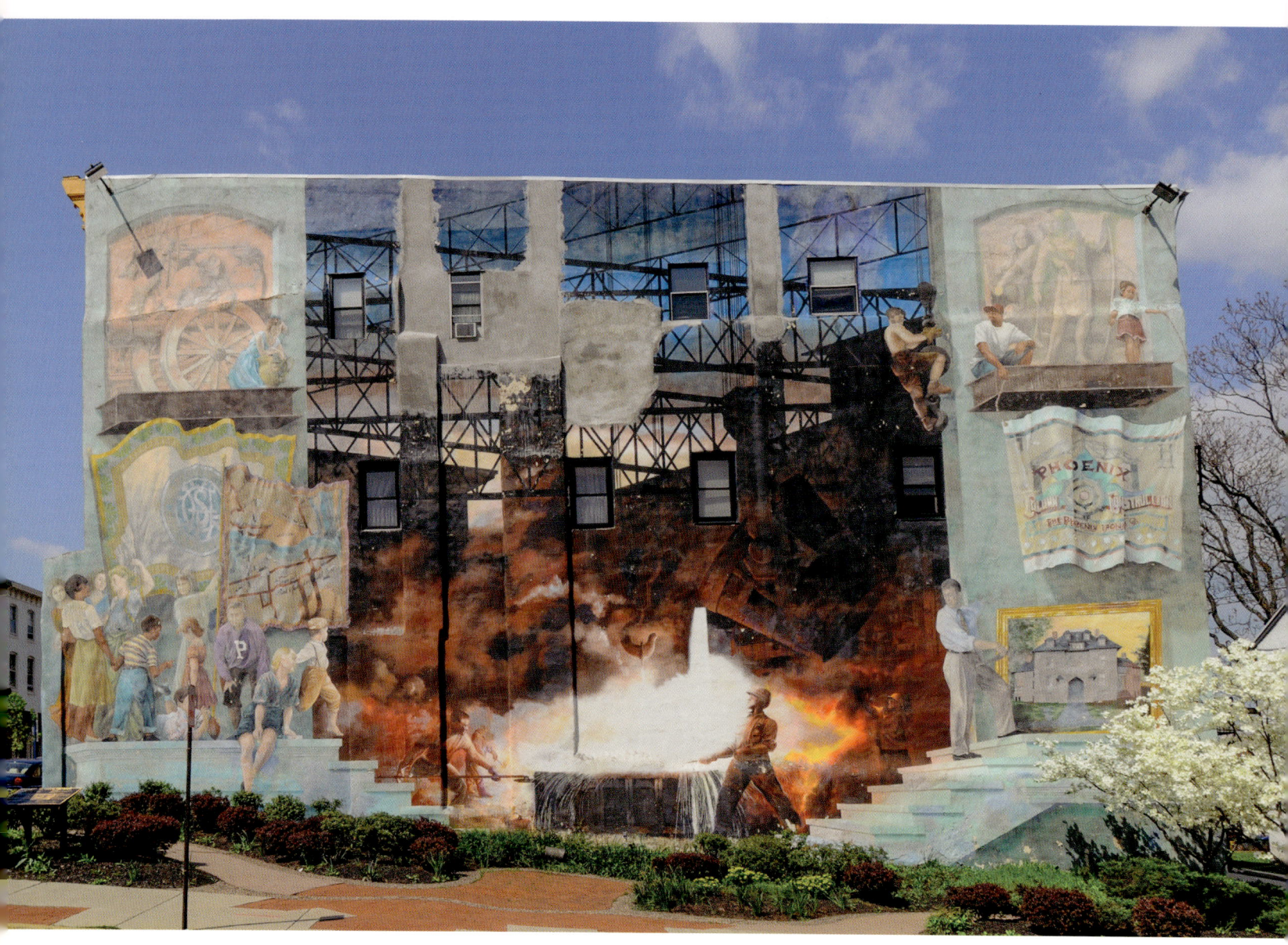

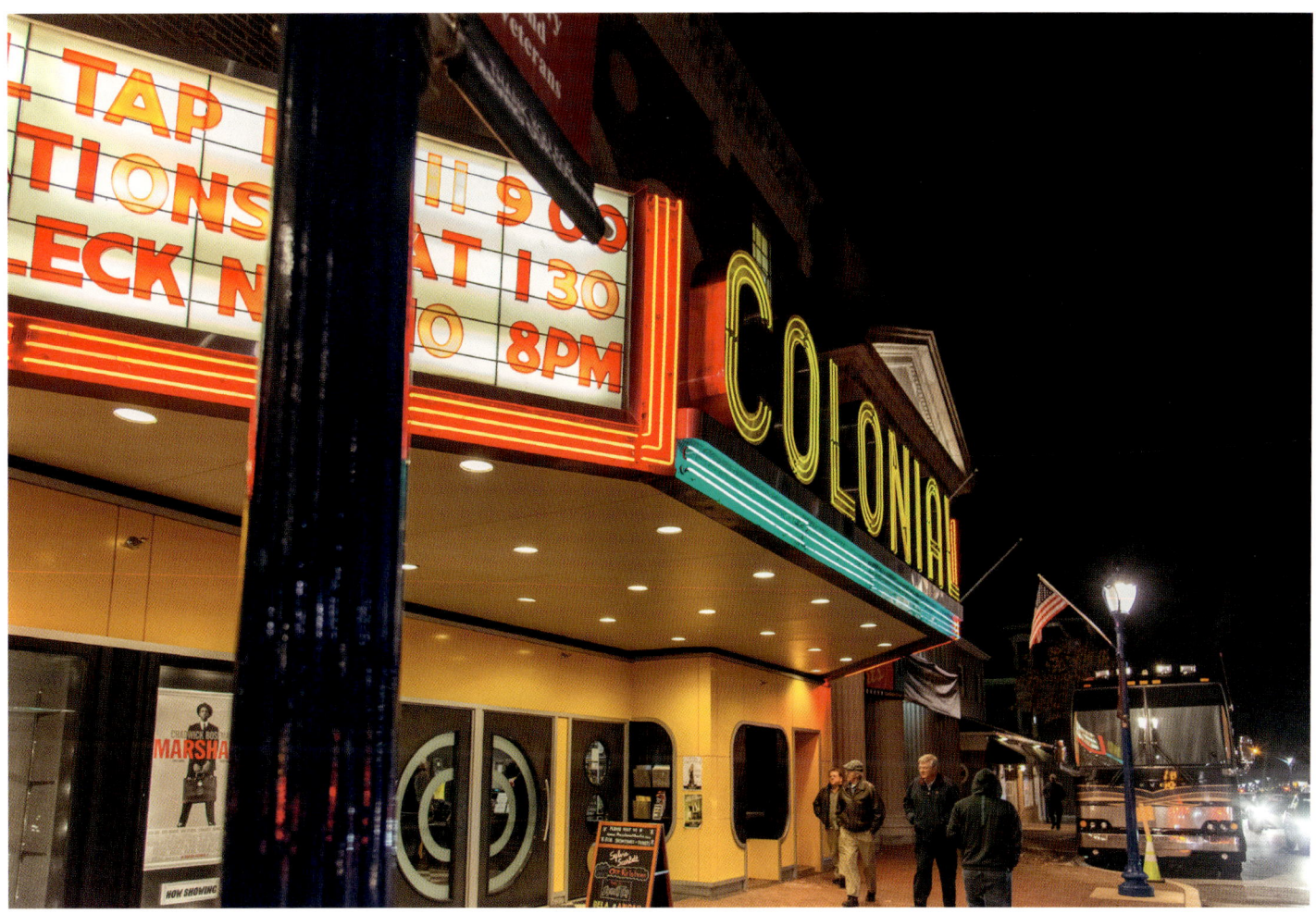

Phoenixville
Originally called Manovan, Phoenixville owes its growth to its waterways—the Schuylkill River for transportation and the fast-moving French Creek for mill power.

Phoenixville
The town was the location of the Phoenix Iron Works and the well-known Etruscan Majolica pottery made by Griffen, Smith & Hill.

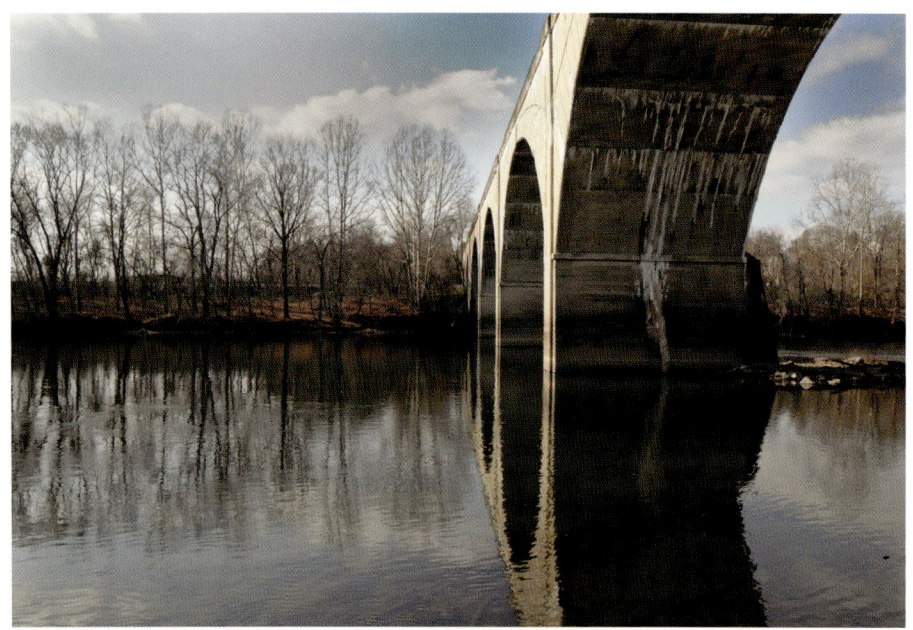

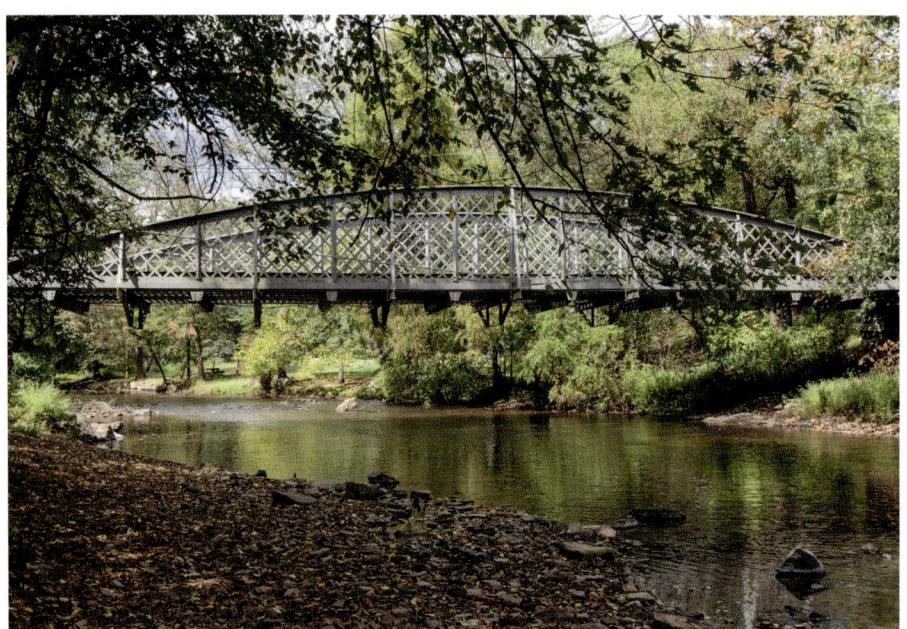

Phoenixville
The bridge of the former Reading Railroad spans the Schuylkill River.

Kimberton, East Pikeland Township
The historically significant Hare's Hill Road Bridge dates to 1869.

West Vincent Township
Sheeder-Hall Covered Bridge across French Creek

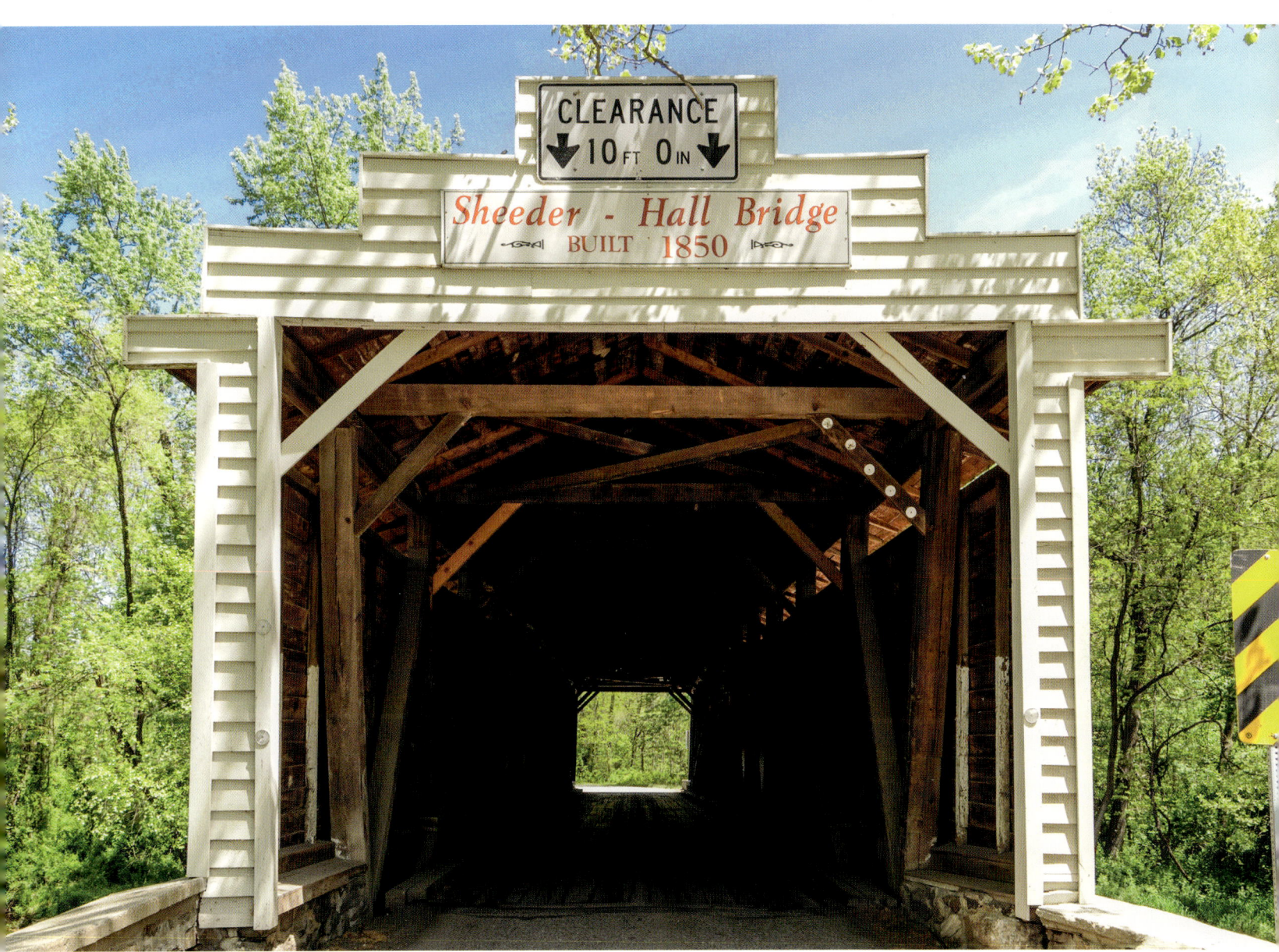

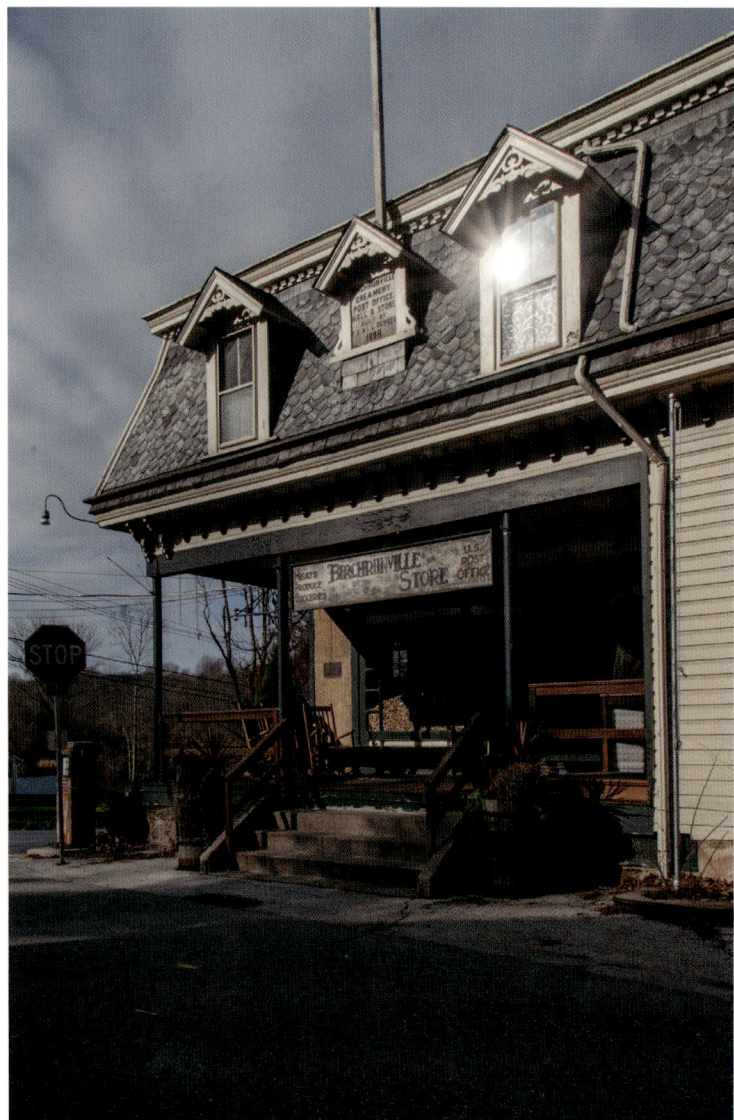
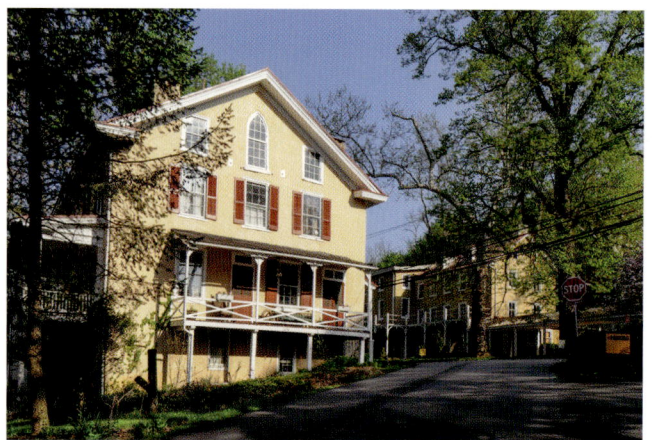
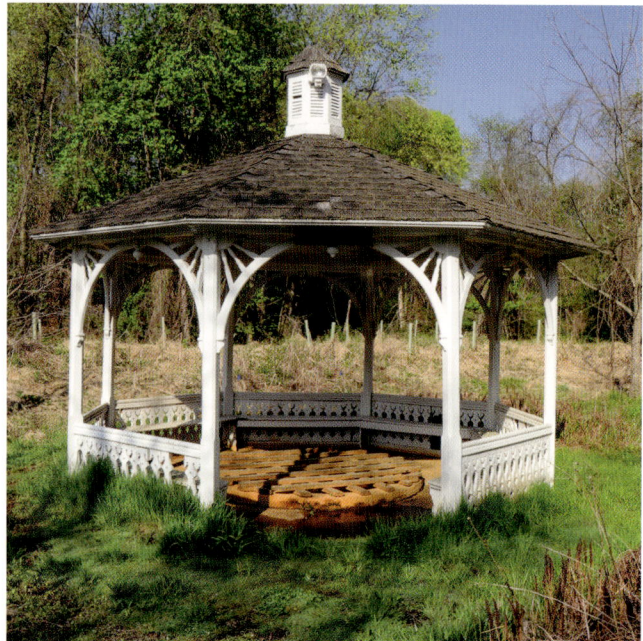

West Vincent Township
Birchrunville General Store, convenience shopping the old-fashioned way

West Pikeland Township
Yellow Springs dates back to the eighteenth century and was a spa built around the mineral springs.

West Pikeland Township
Pike's Land was the first name given to a grant of 10,000 acres by William Penn to Joseph Pike from County Cork, Ireland, in 1705.

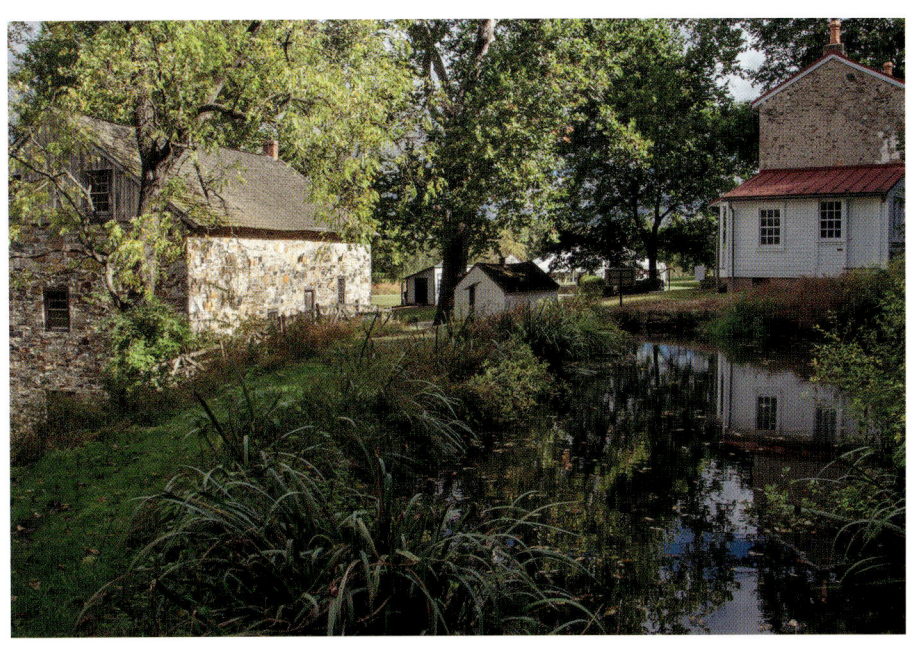

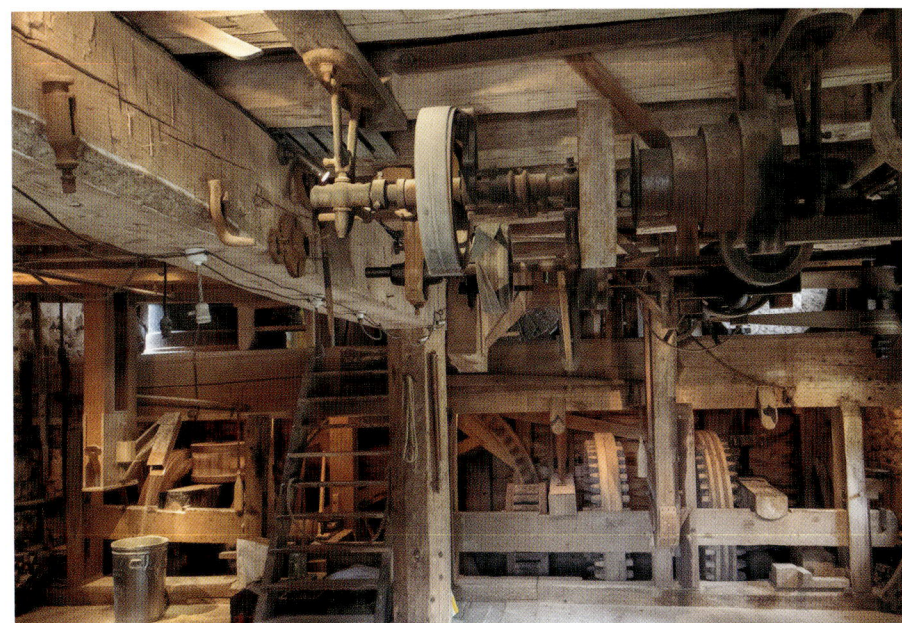

West Pikeland Township
Mill at Anselma

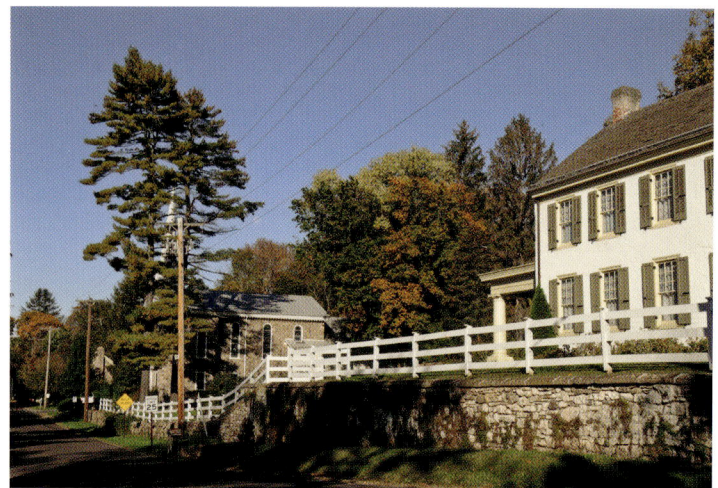

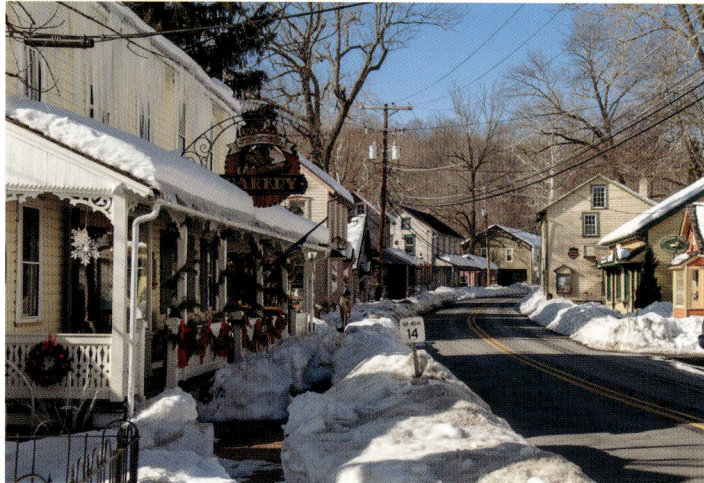

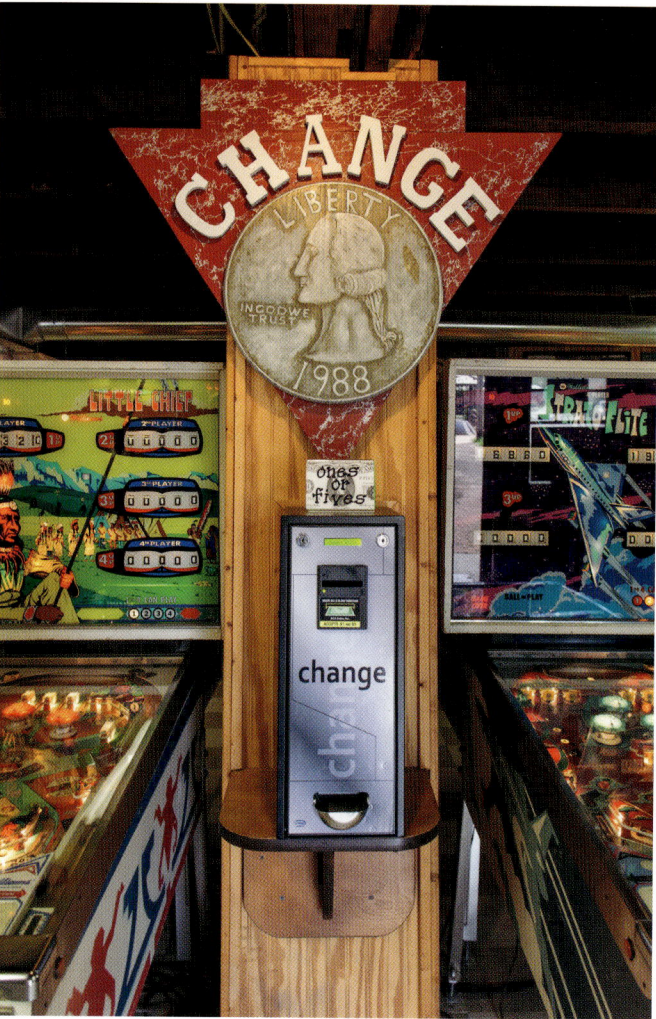

South Coventry Township
Coventryville

Warwick Township
St. Peter's Village is on the National Register of Historic Places and is located on French Creek in Warwick Township. It was a late-nineteenth-century industrial company village, which served iron-mining and granite-quarrying businesses. The St. Peter's Inn was the first building to have been erected.

Warwick Township
Pinball Arcade Museum, St. Peter's Village

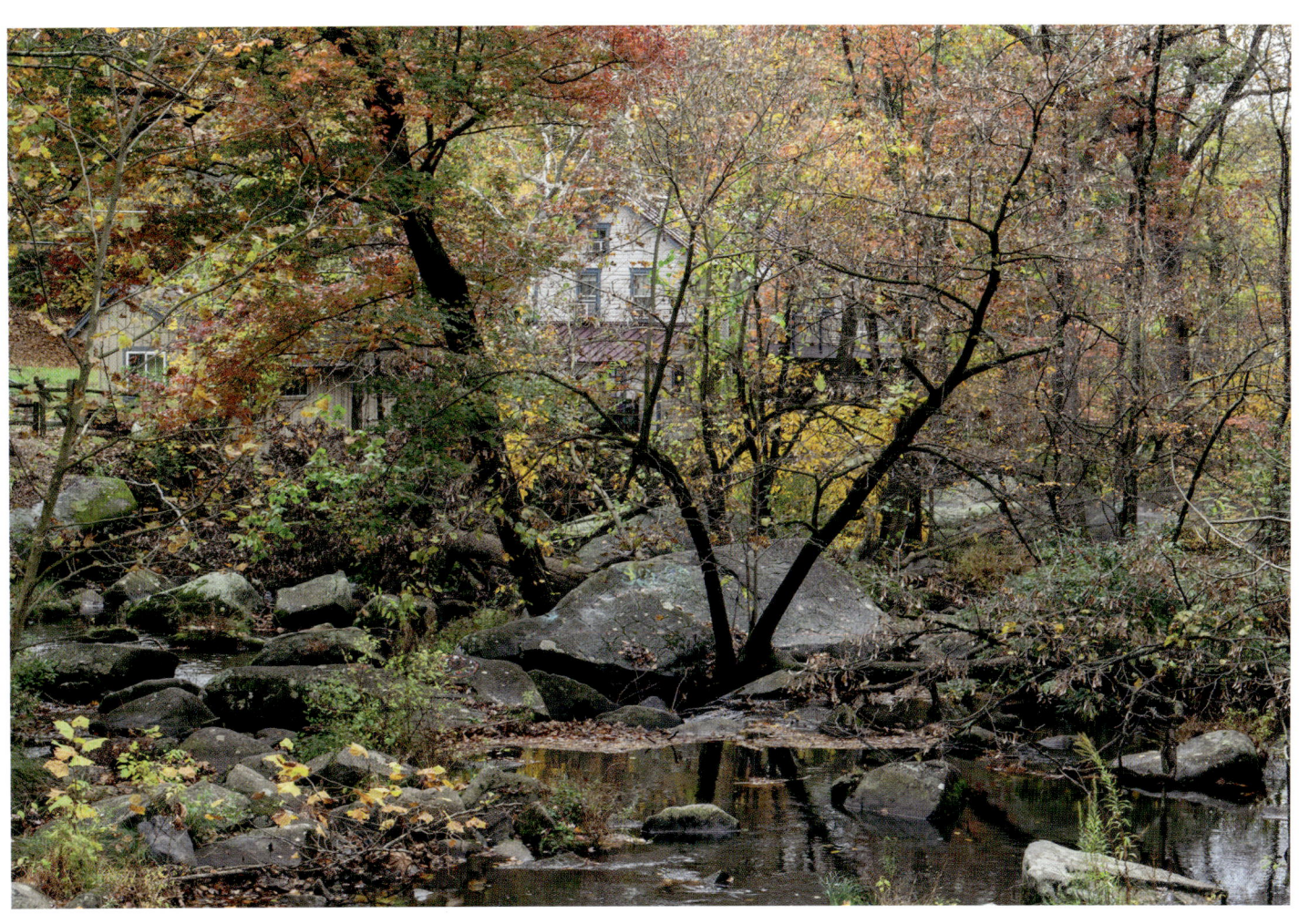

Warwick Township
French Creek, St. Peter's Village

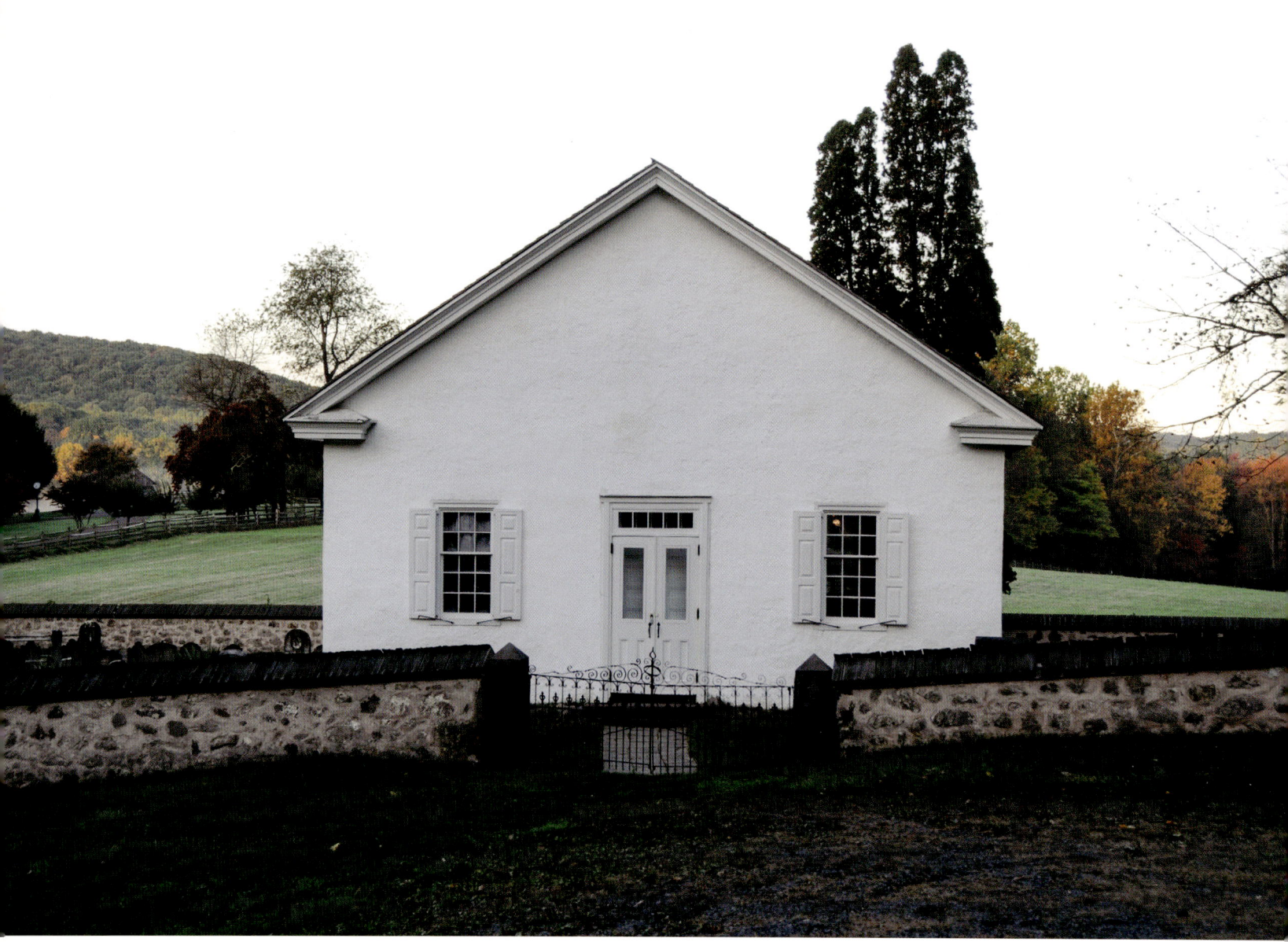

Bethesda Church, Warwick Township
Warwick Township was carved out of Nantmeal and named for the Warwick Iron Works, which were within its boundaries.

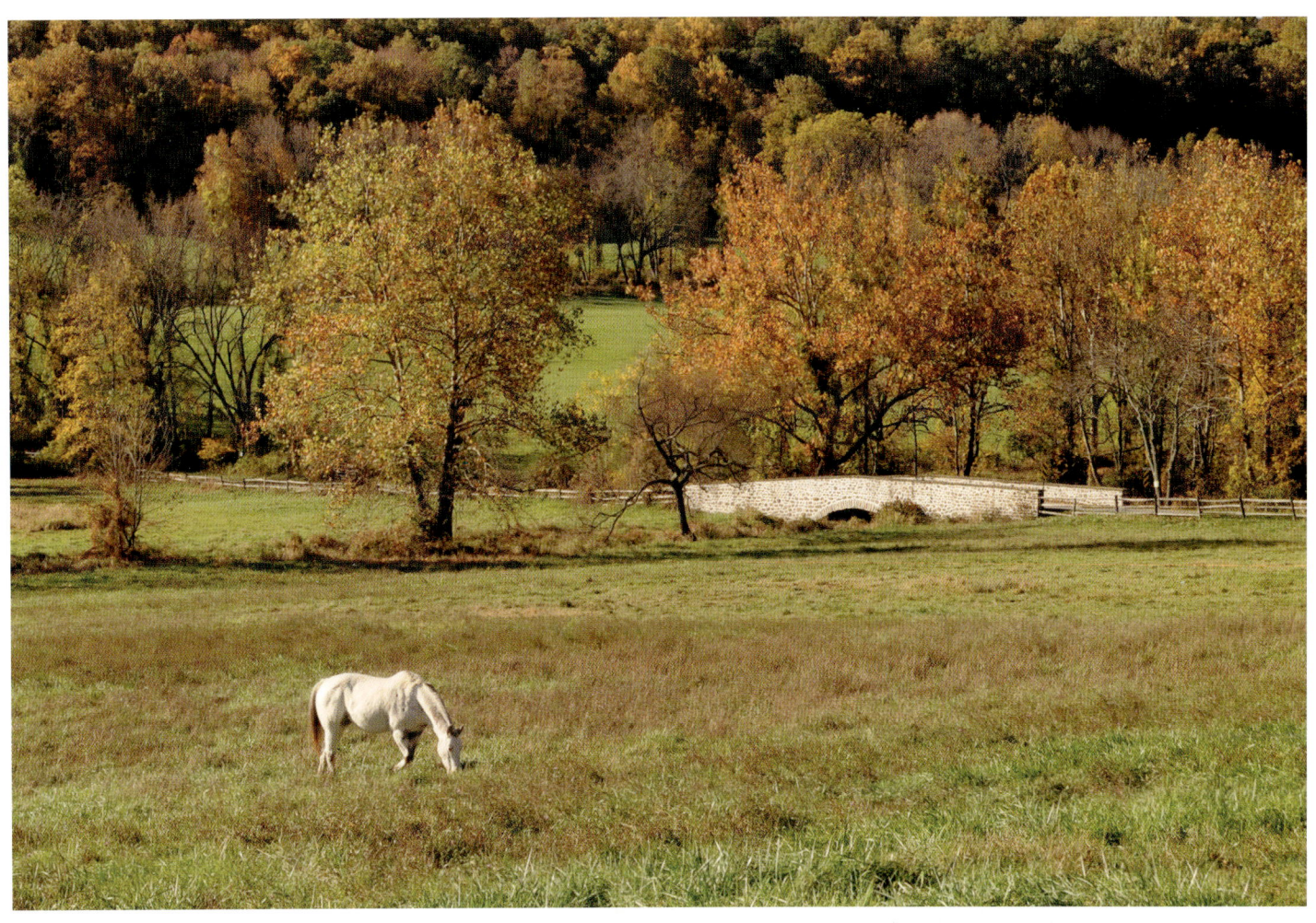

Warwick Township

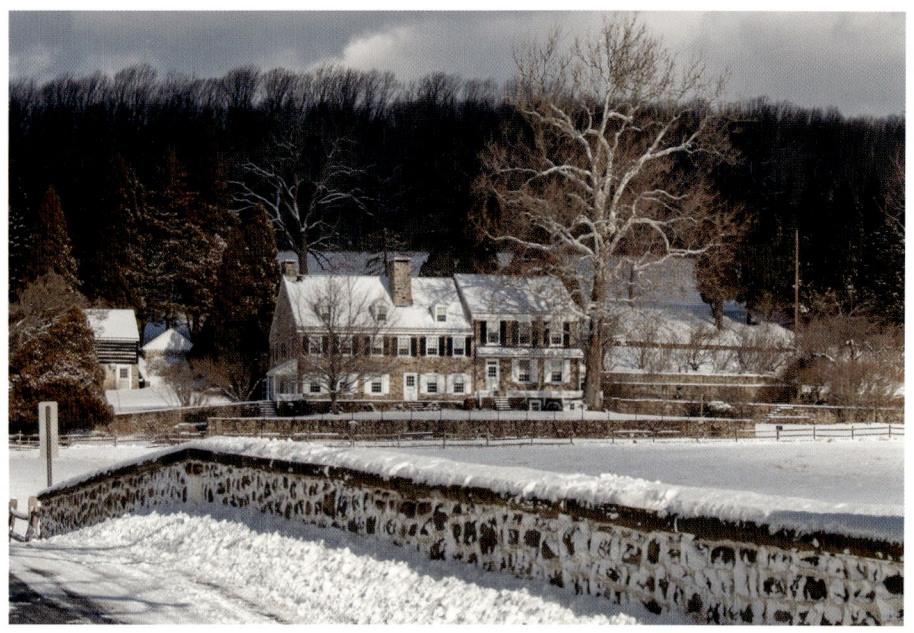

Warwick Township
Overlooking Warwick Furnace Farms
and ruins of the Warwick Furnace

Honey Brook Township

West Fallowfield Township

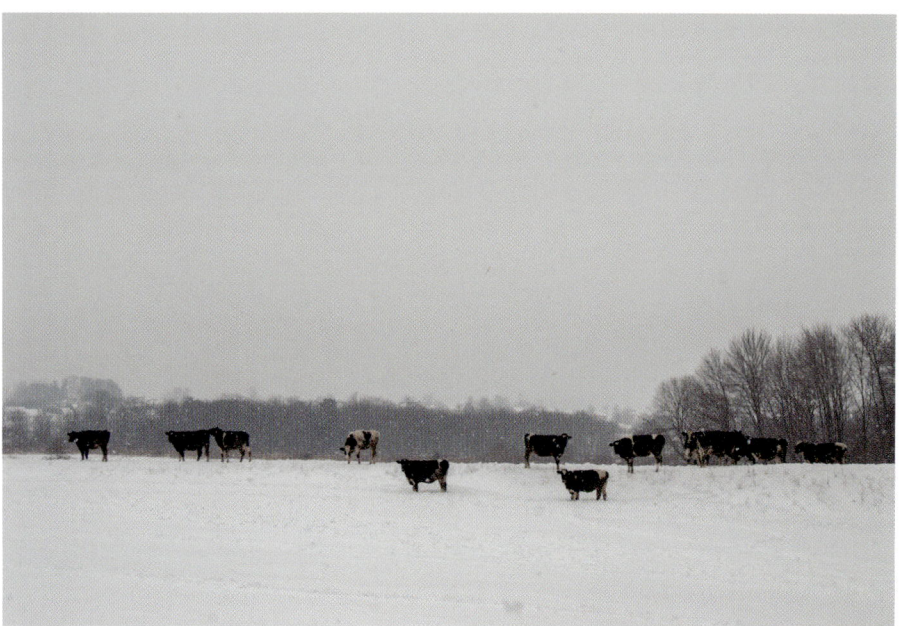

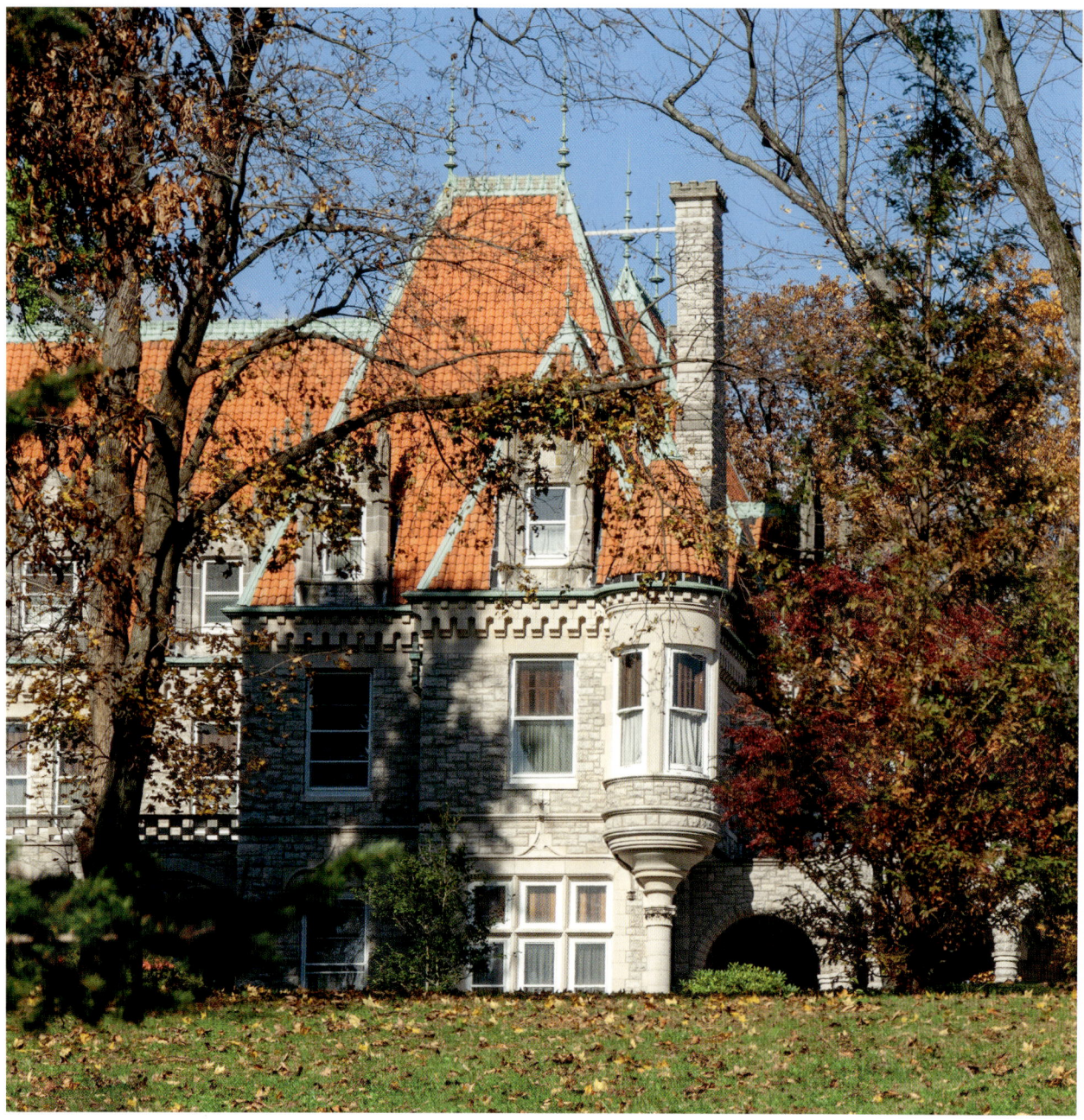

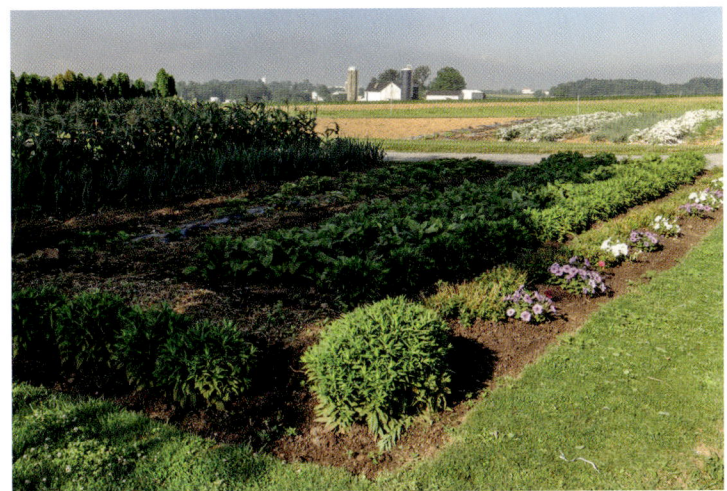

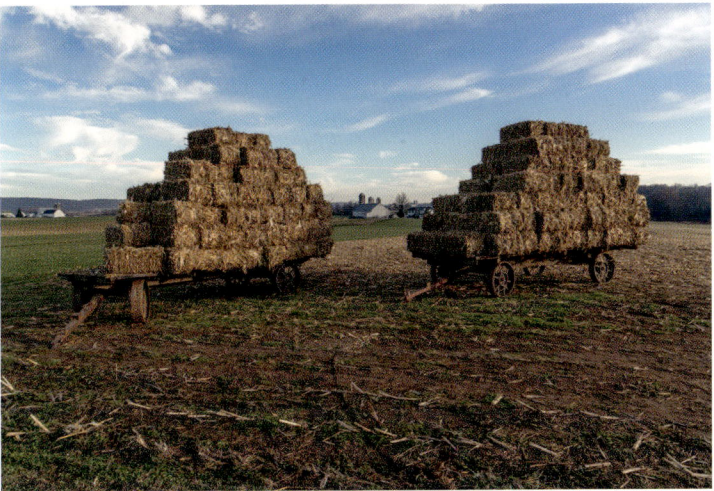

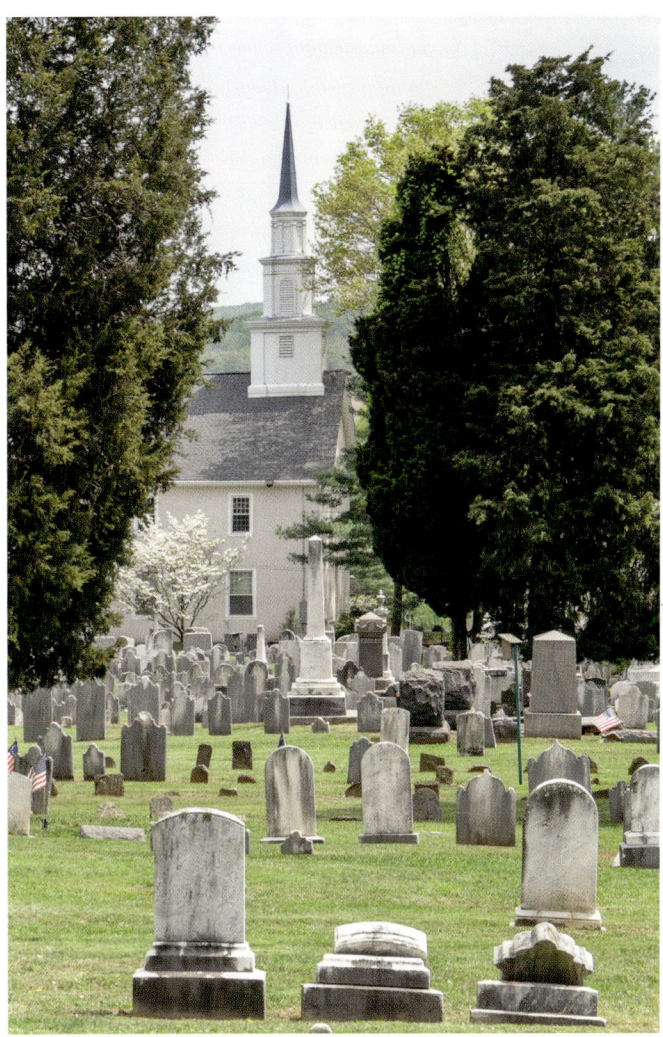

West Nantmeal Township
The St. Mary of Providence mansion was built by Joseph D. Potts in the late nineteenth century and now serves as a retreat center and home for senior citizens. Nantmeal, which means sweet water, was settled by Quakers who migrated from Nantmel in Wales.

Honey Brook Township

East Pikeland Township
St. Peter's Church

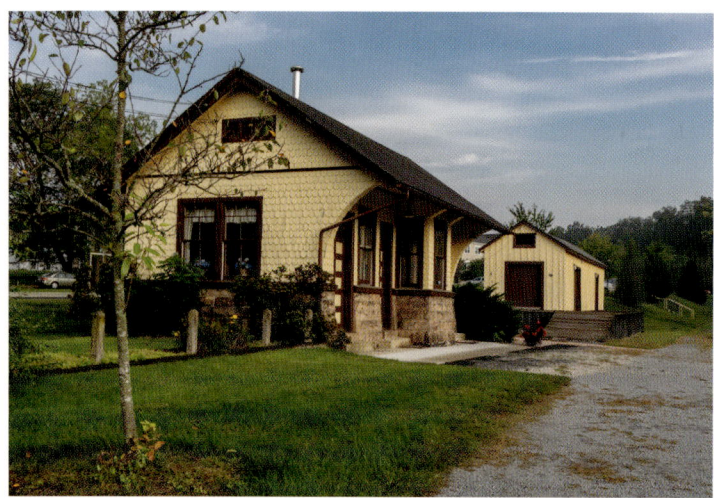

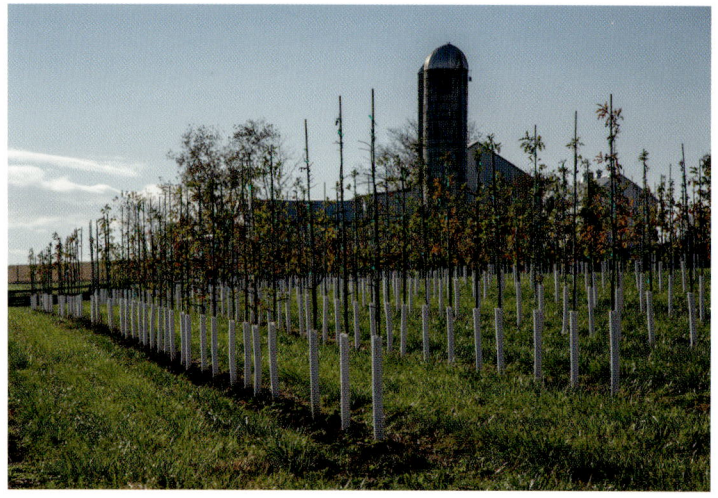

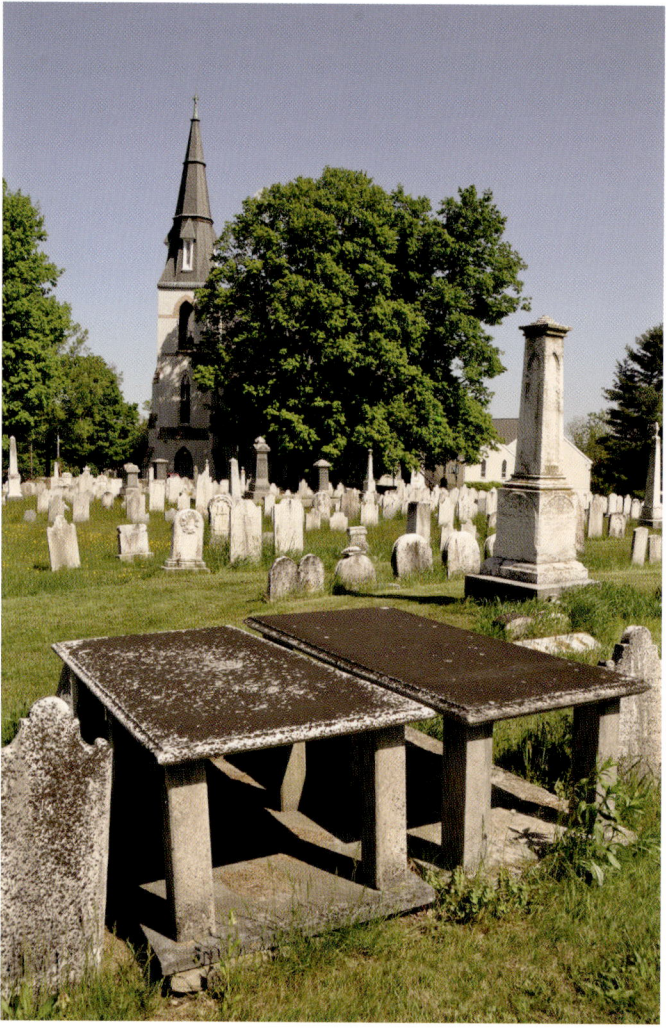

Elverson
Trains used to run through here.

Honey Brook Township

West Brandywine Township
Forks of the Brandywine Presbyterian Church

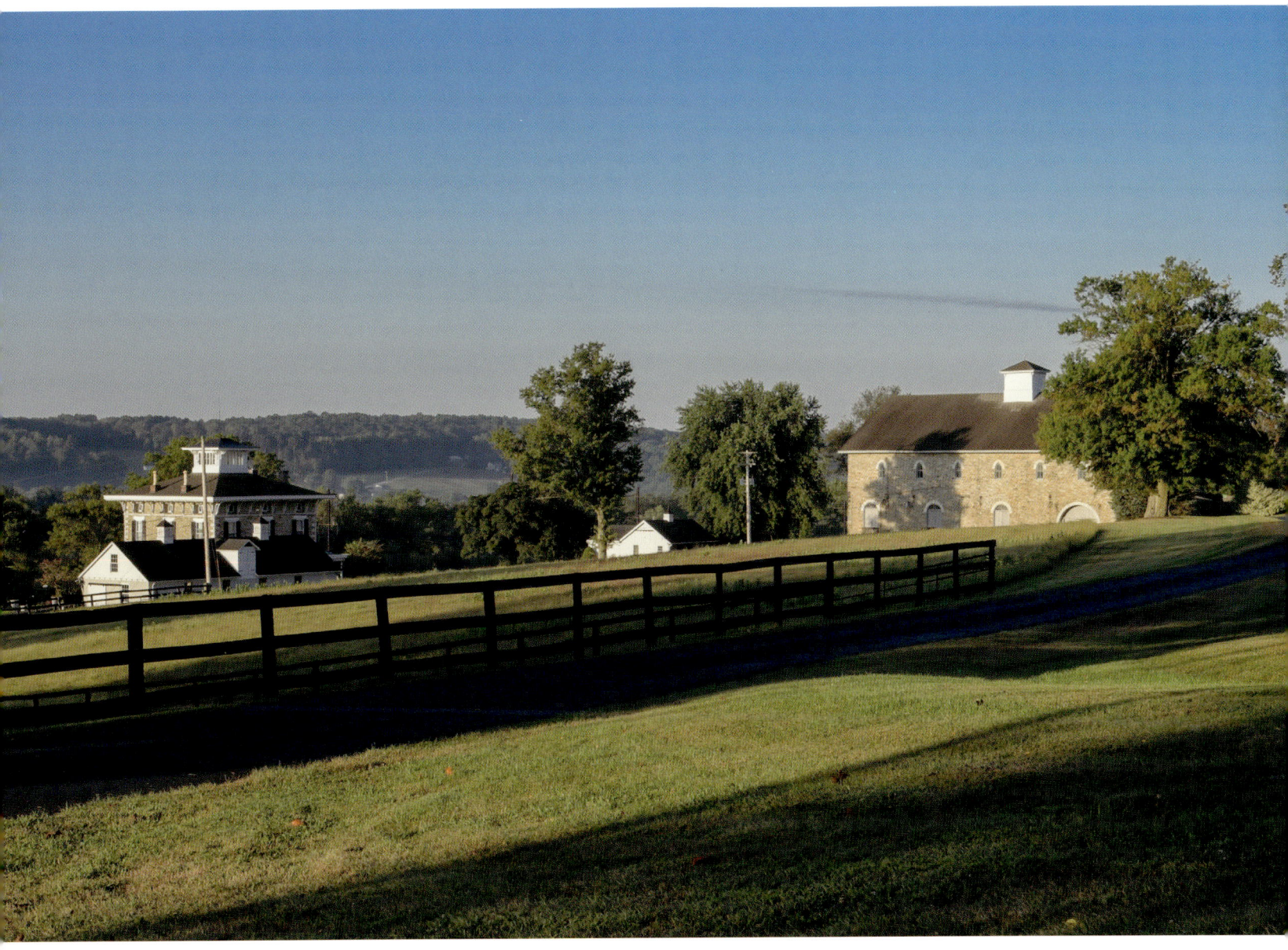

Atglen

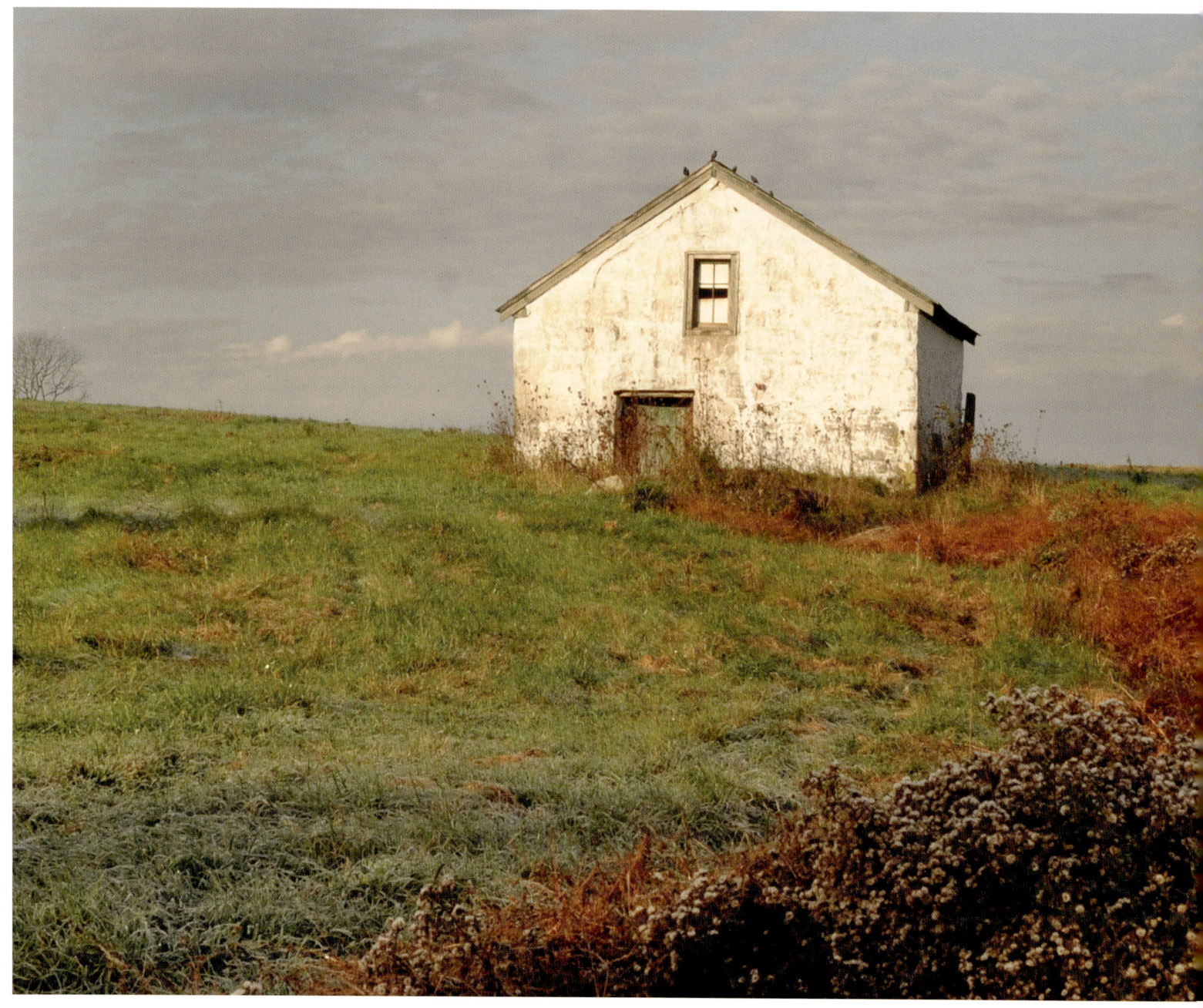

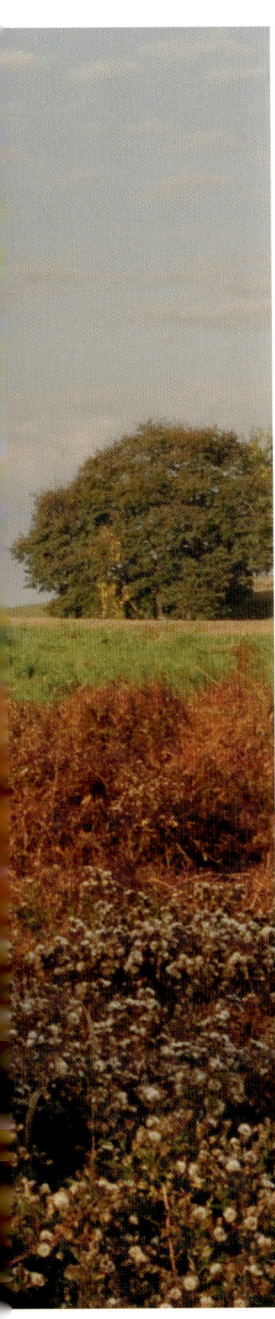

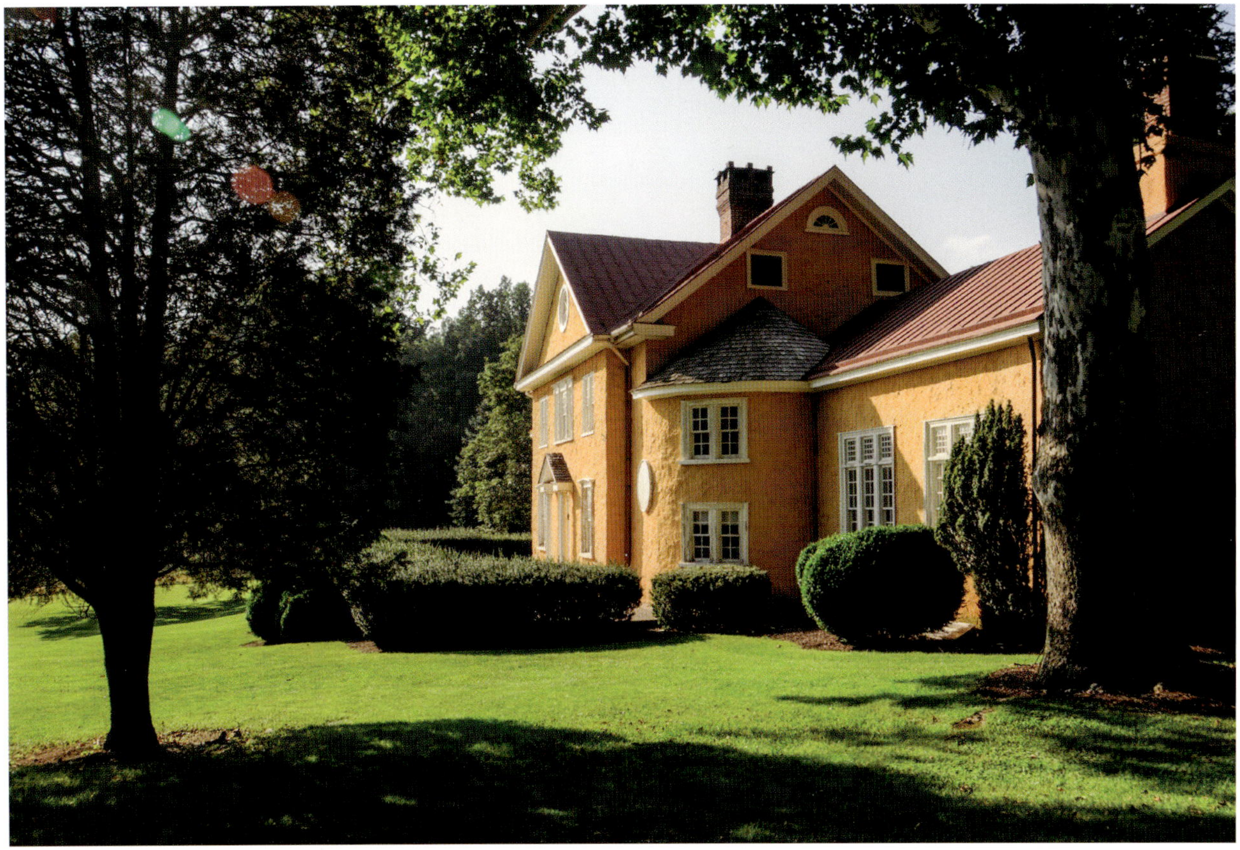

East Brandywine Township
Springhouse

West Caln Township
Hibernia Mansion, Hibernia County Park

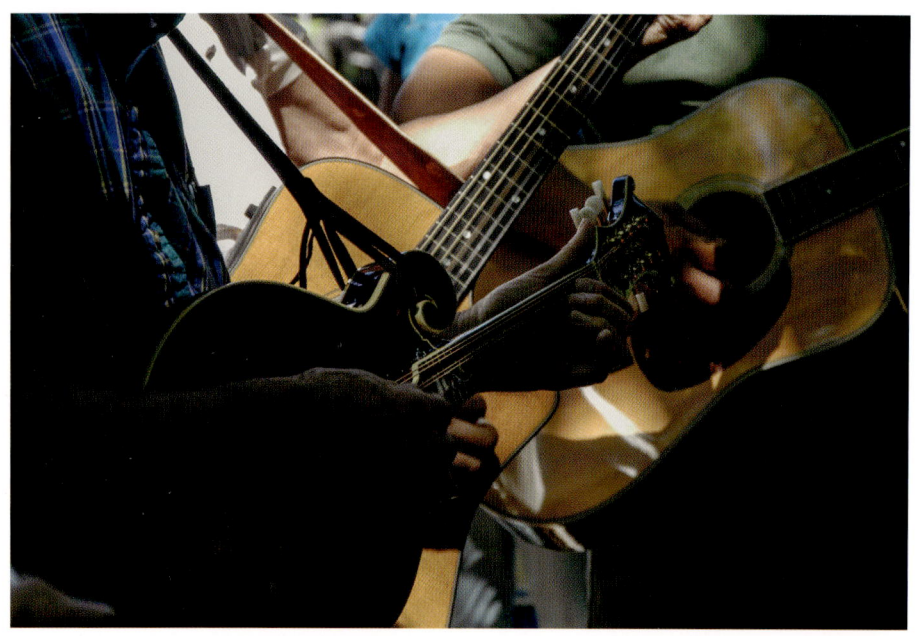

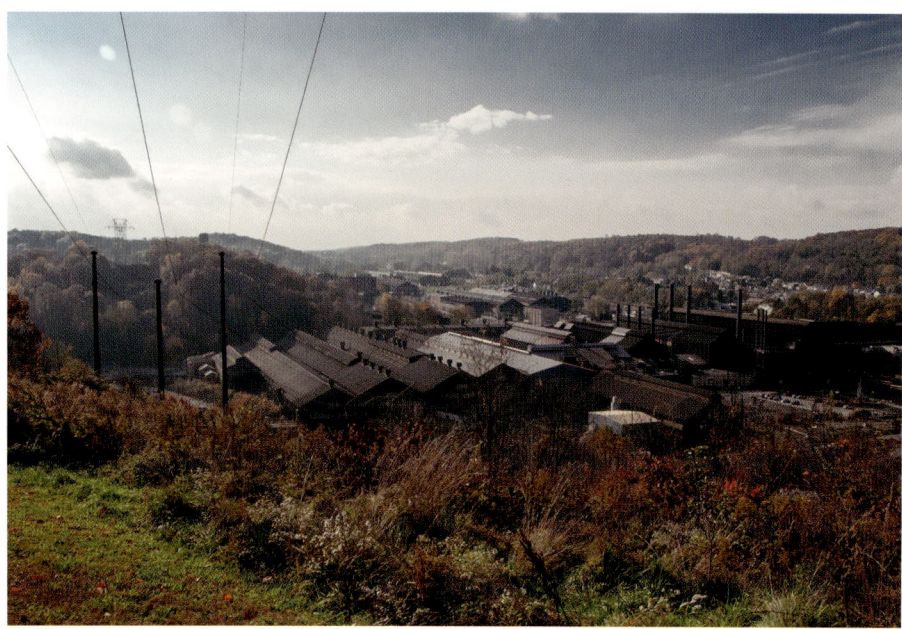

West Caln Township
Annual Old Fiddlers' Picnic, Hibernia County Park

Coatesville
ArcelorMittal (formerly Lukens) Steel Plants

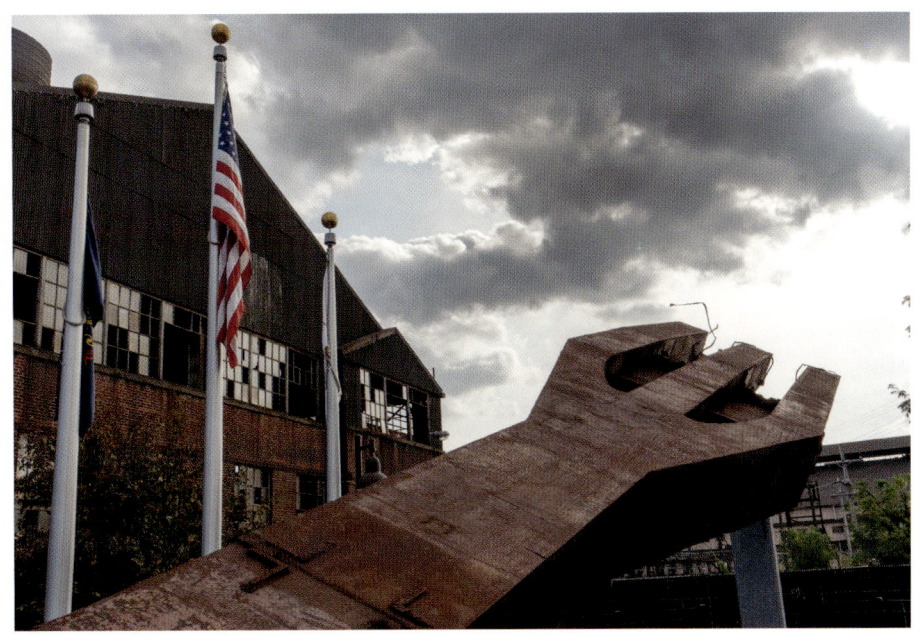

Lukens Steel Historic District, Coatesville
The specialized steel for the World Trade Center's lower structure came from here.

Coatesville
Coatesville Invitational Vintage Grand Prix

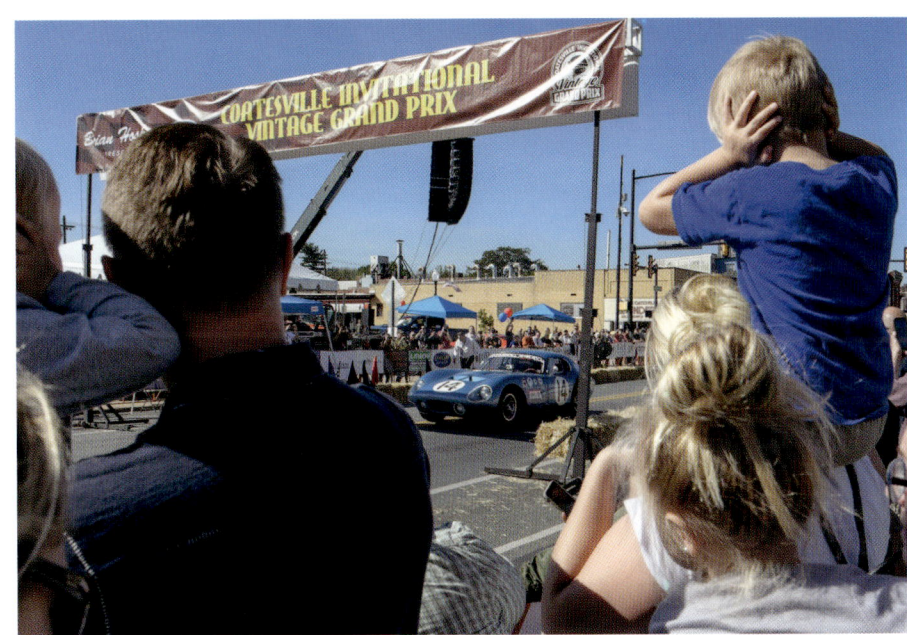

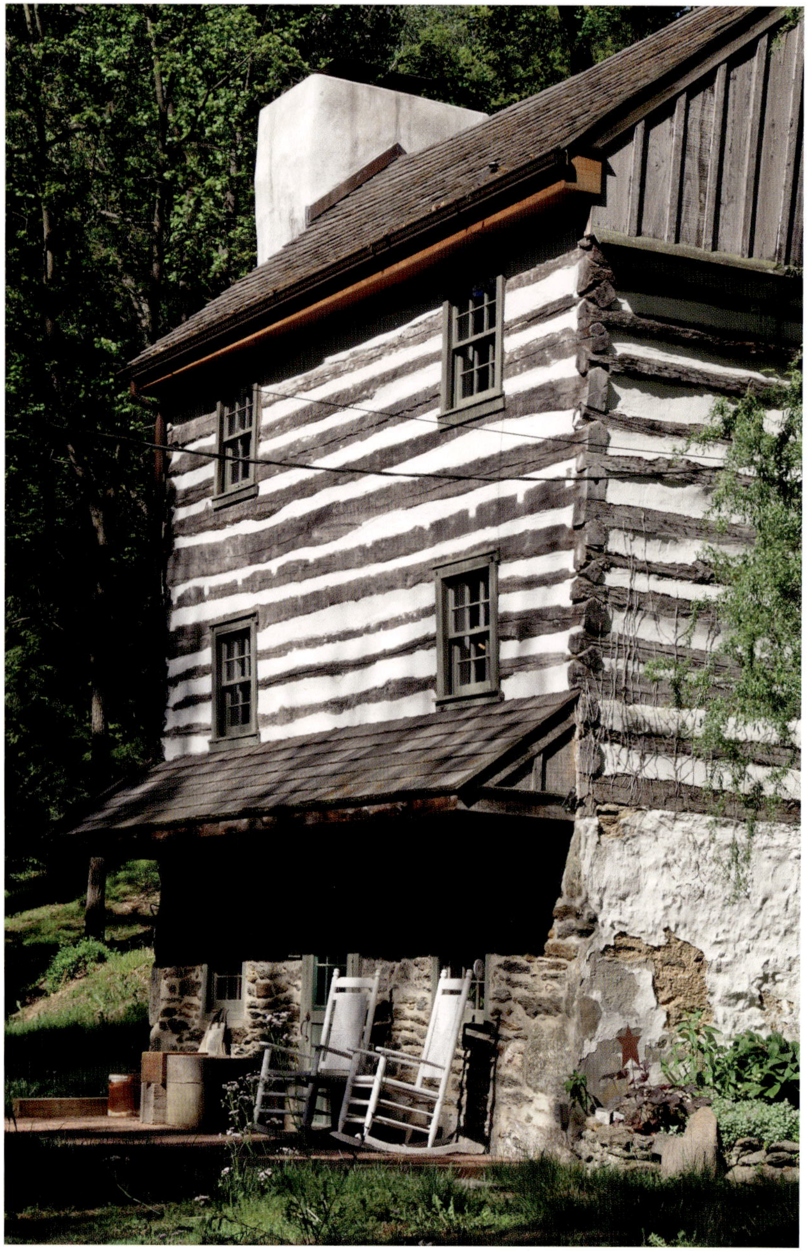

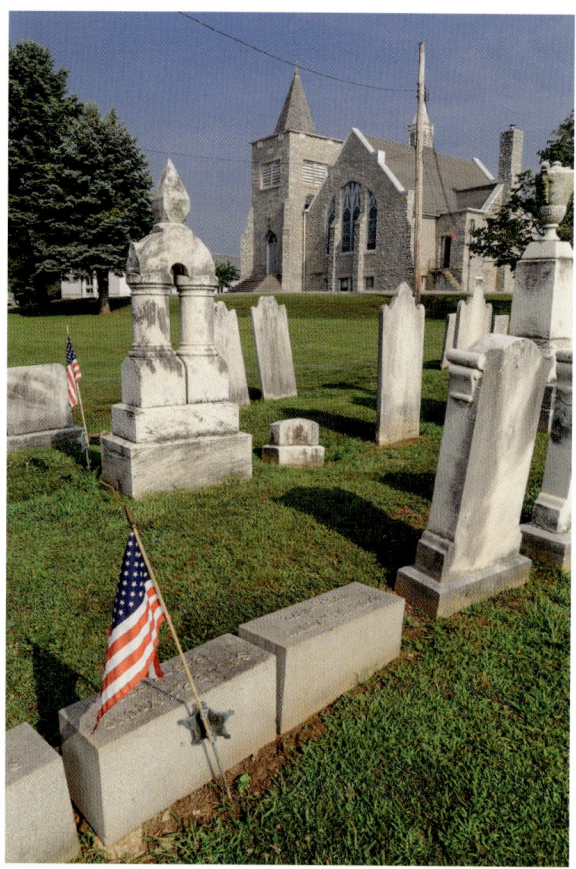
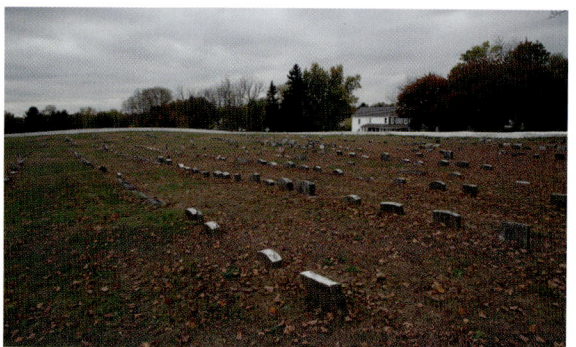

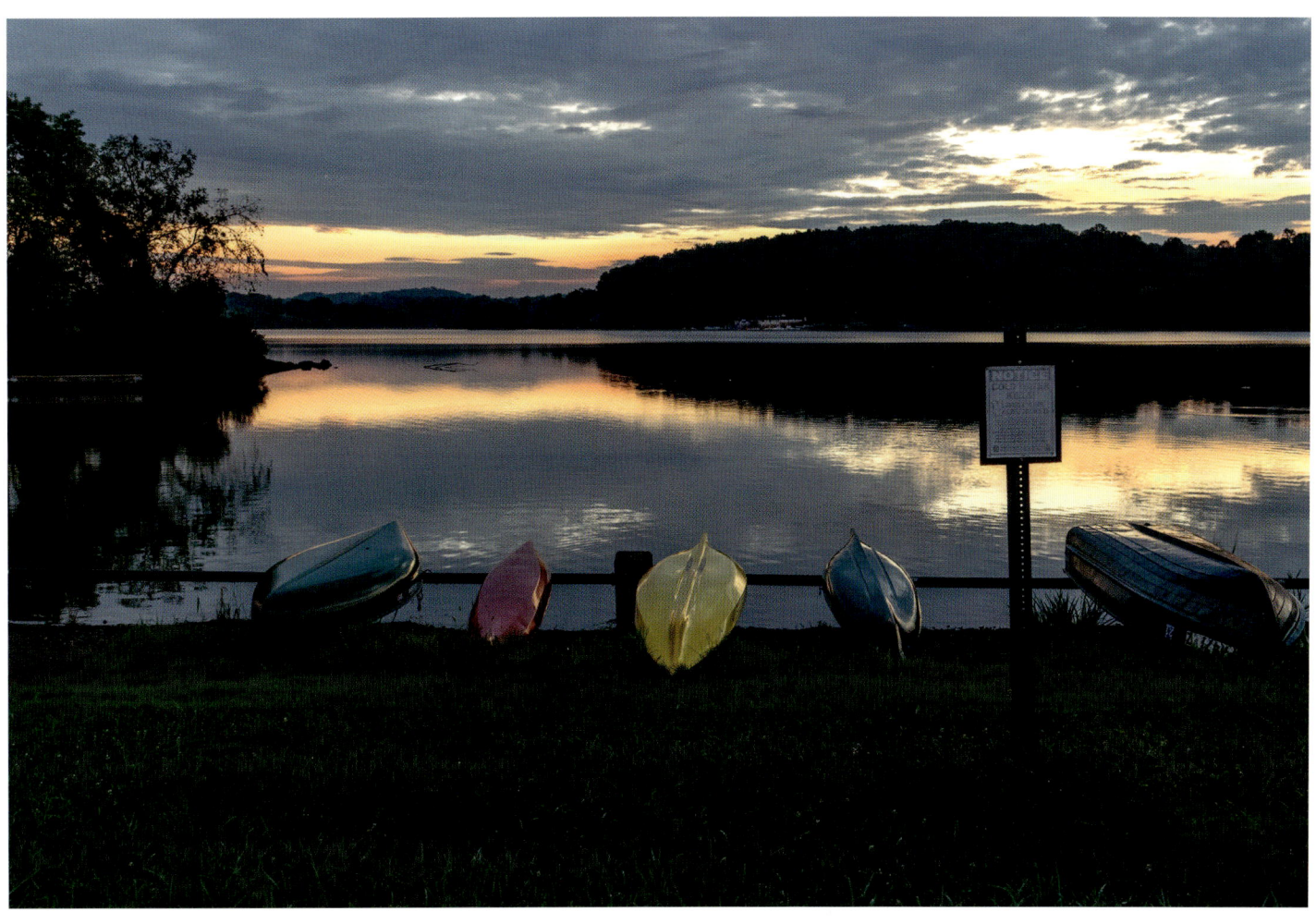

East Fallowfield Township
The Fallowfields (East and West) take their names from Launcelot Fallowfield, who came from England and purchased the land from William Penn.

East Fallowfield
Hephzibah Baptist Church

East Fallowfield
Ercildoun

Marsh Creek State Park, Upper Uwchlan Township
Uwchlan means "land above the valley."

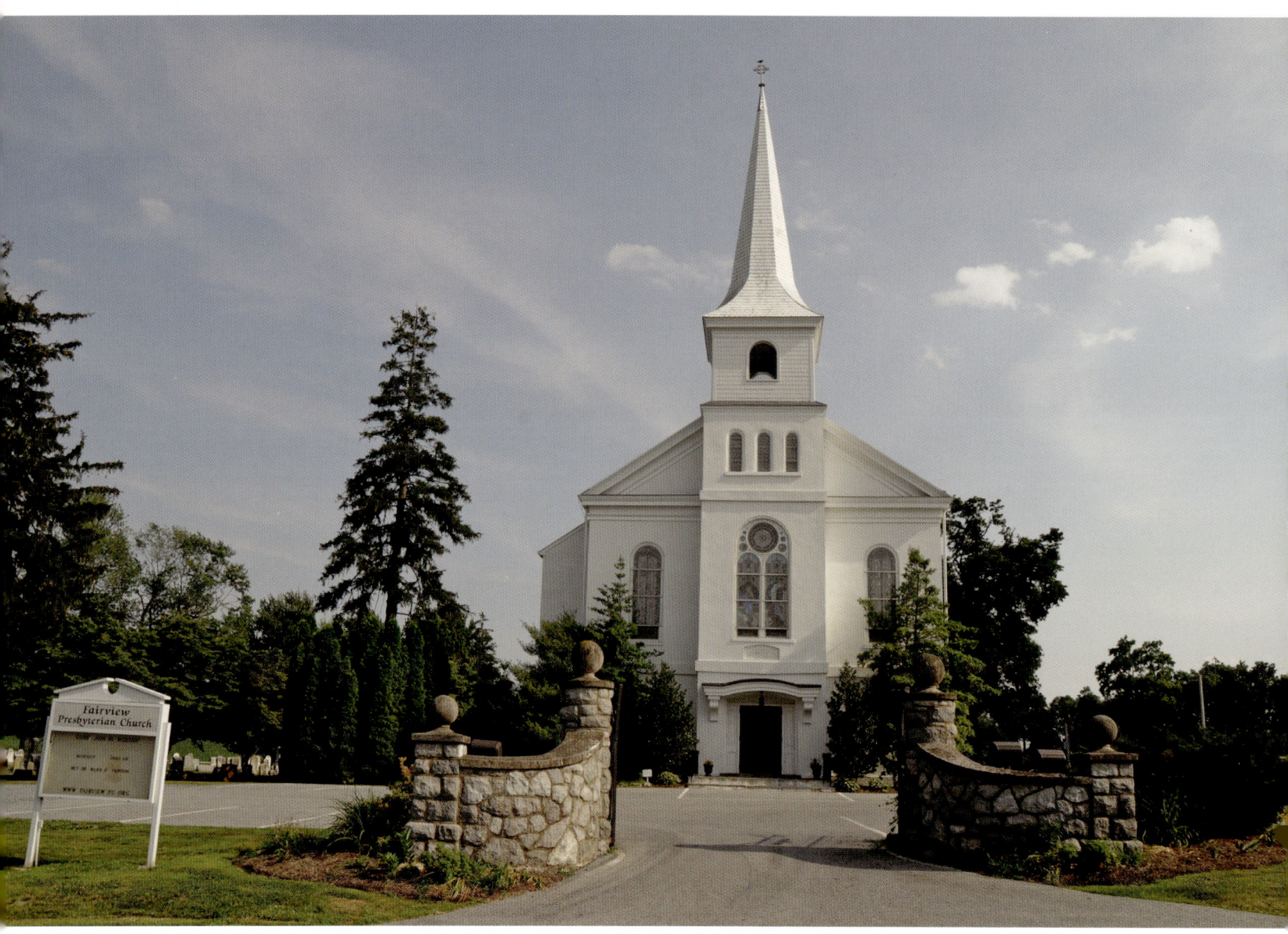

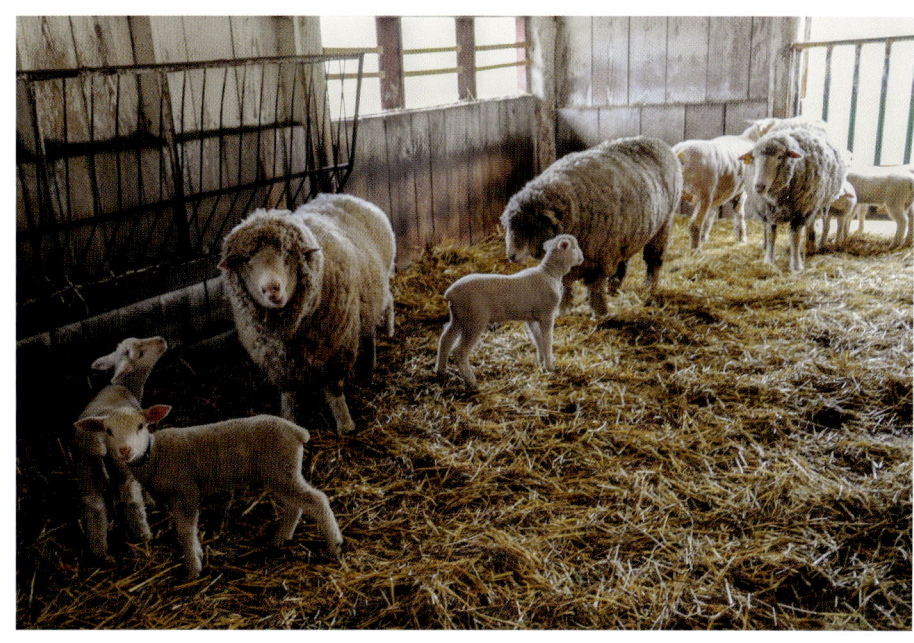

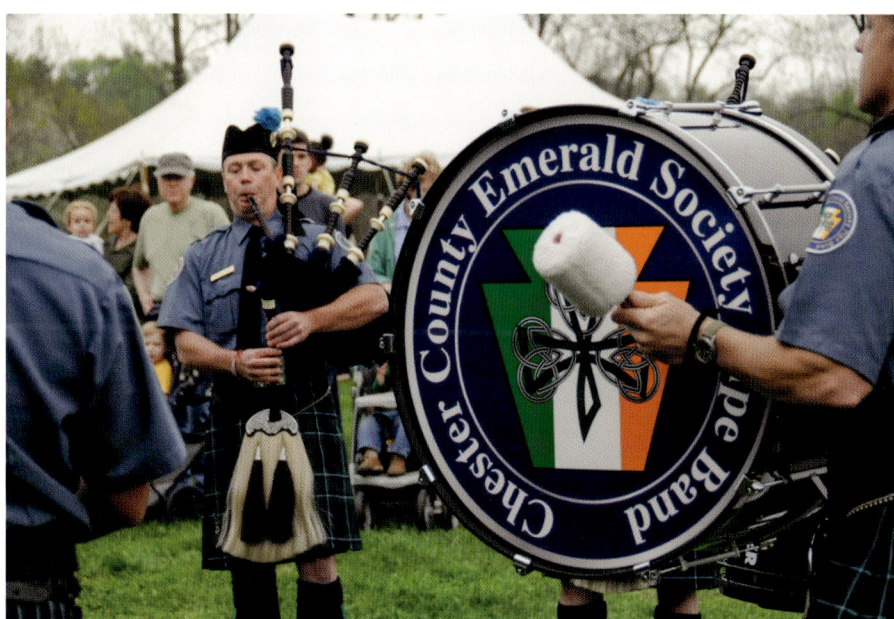

Wallace Township
Fairview Presbyterian Church

Wallace Township
Springton Manor Farm (county park), formerly the Manor of Springton

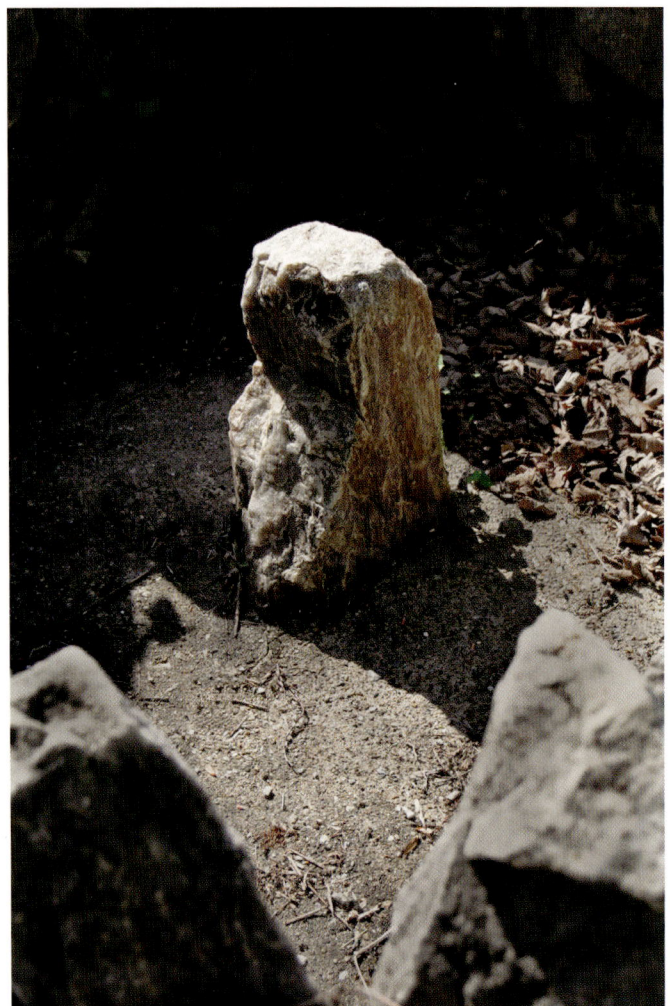
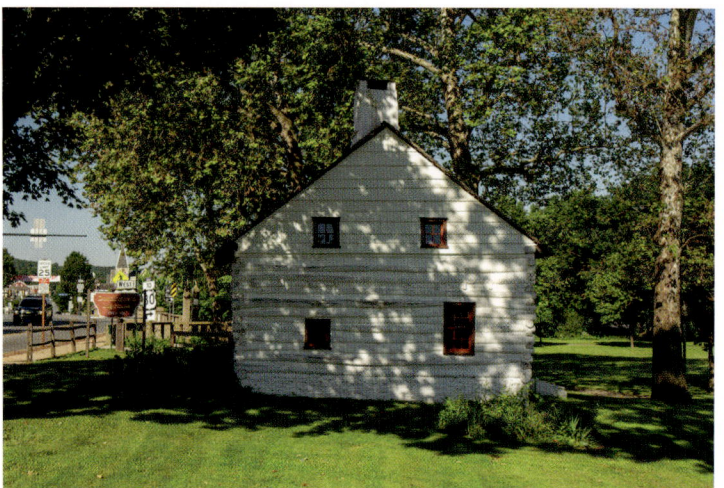
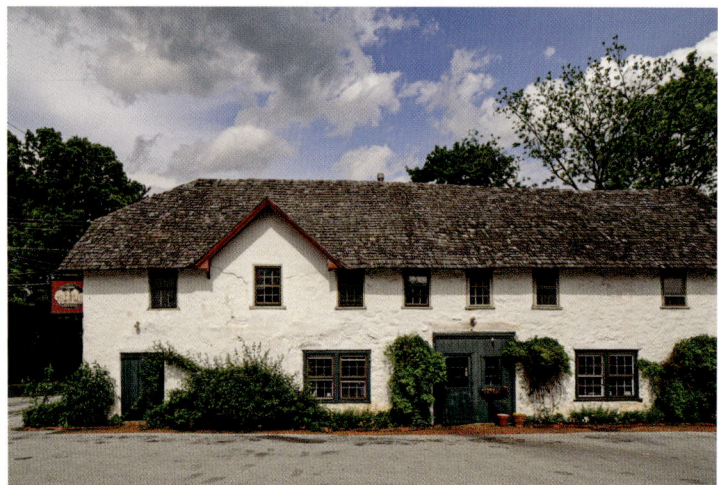

Newlin Township
The Stargazers Stone was set in 1764 by Messrs. Mason and Dixon and marks an important astronomical observation point for setting the latitude of their famous line 15 miles to the south.

Downingtown Log House
The town was originally named Milltown, reflecting the number of mills that lined Brandywine Creek. Around the time of the American Revolution, Milltown became more commonly known as Downing's Town because Thomas Downing, a 1717 Quaker immigrant from Bradninch, Devon, England, owned a number of those mills.

Marshallton, West Bradford Township
Four Dogs Tavern is reminiscent of an English pub with a thatched roof.

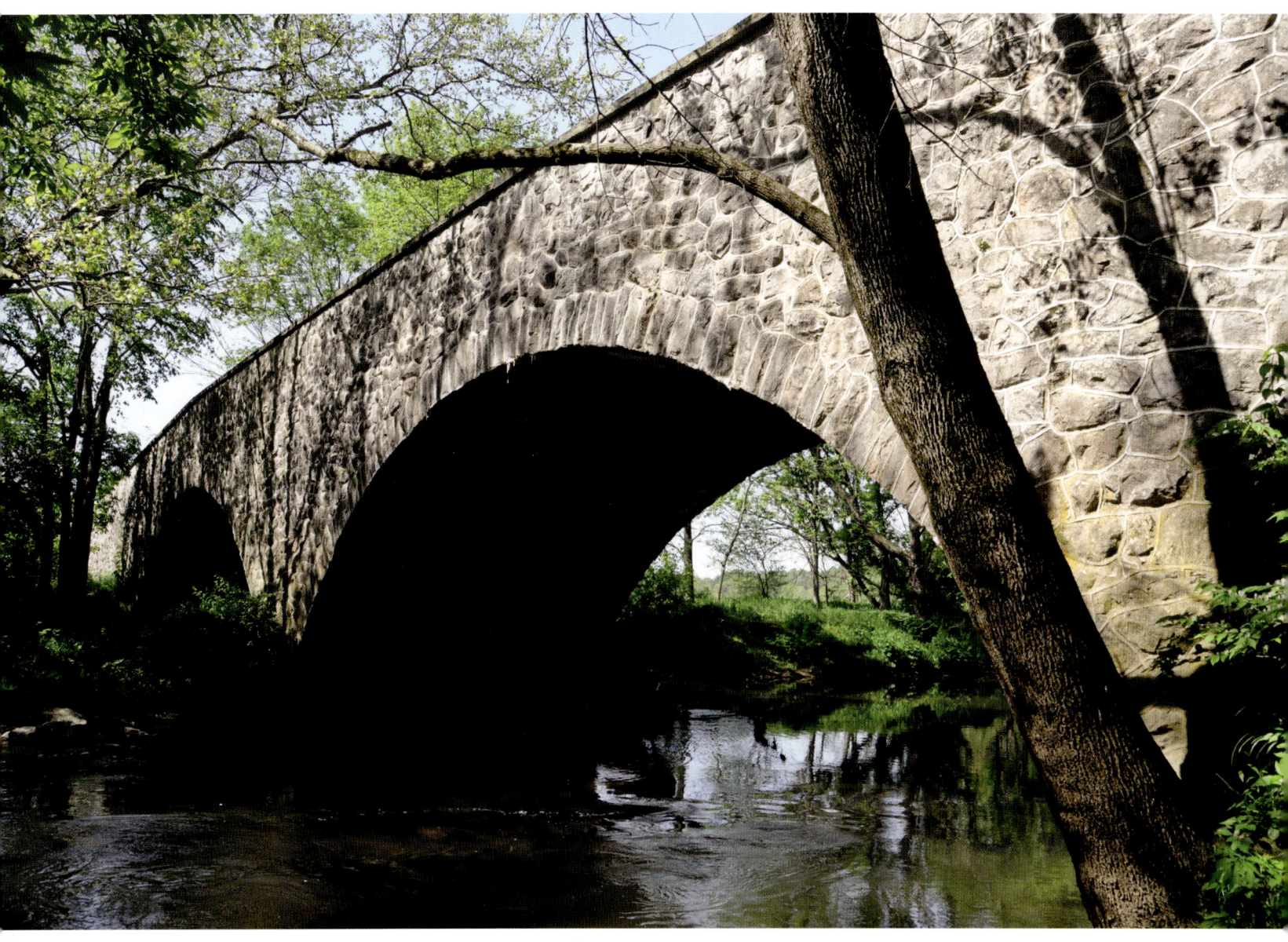

Embreeville, Newlin Township
Farmer's Bridge over Brandywine Creek

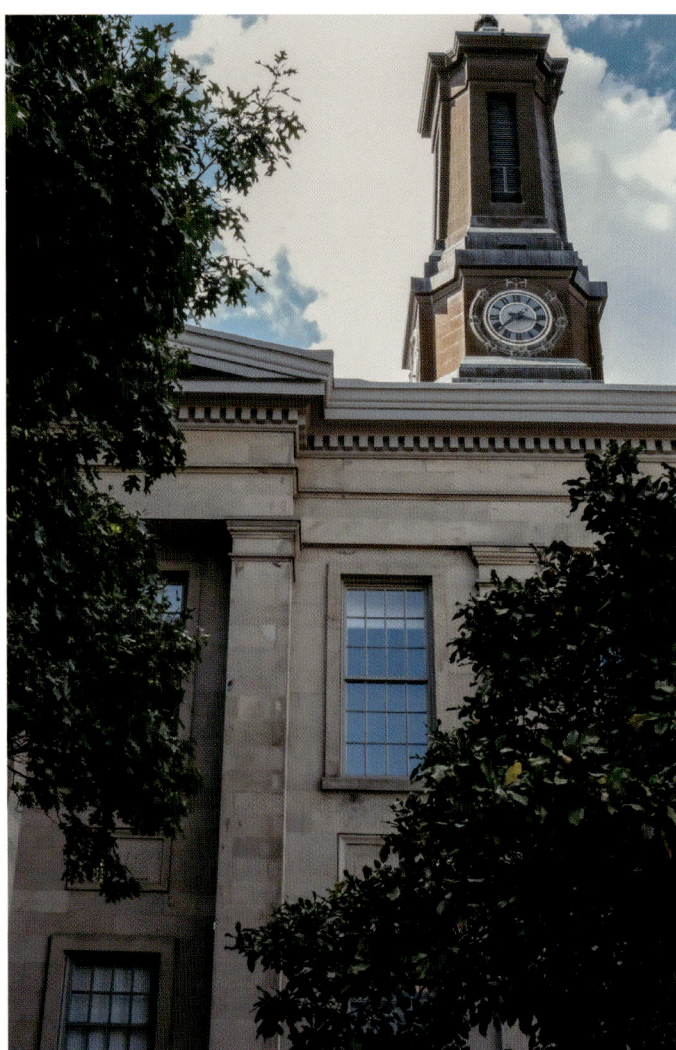
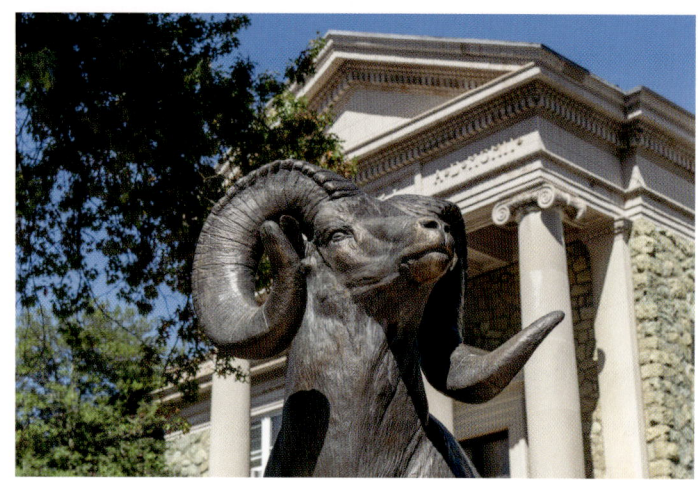

West Chester
The Chester County Courthouse, a classical revival building designed in the 1840s by Thomas U. Walter, one of the architects for the Capitol in Washington, DC

West Chester University

West Chester
West Chester has a vibrant dining and entertainment scene.

West Chester
The town was originally known as Turk's Head after an inn of the same name.

West Chester
Uptown! Knauer Performing Arts Center

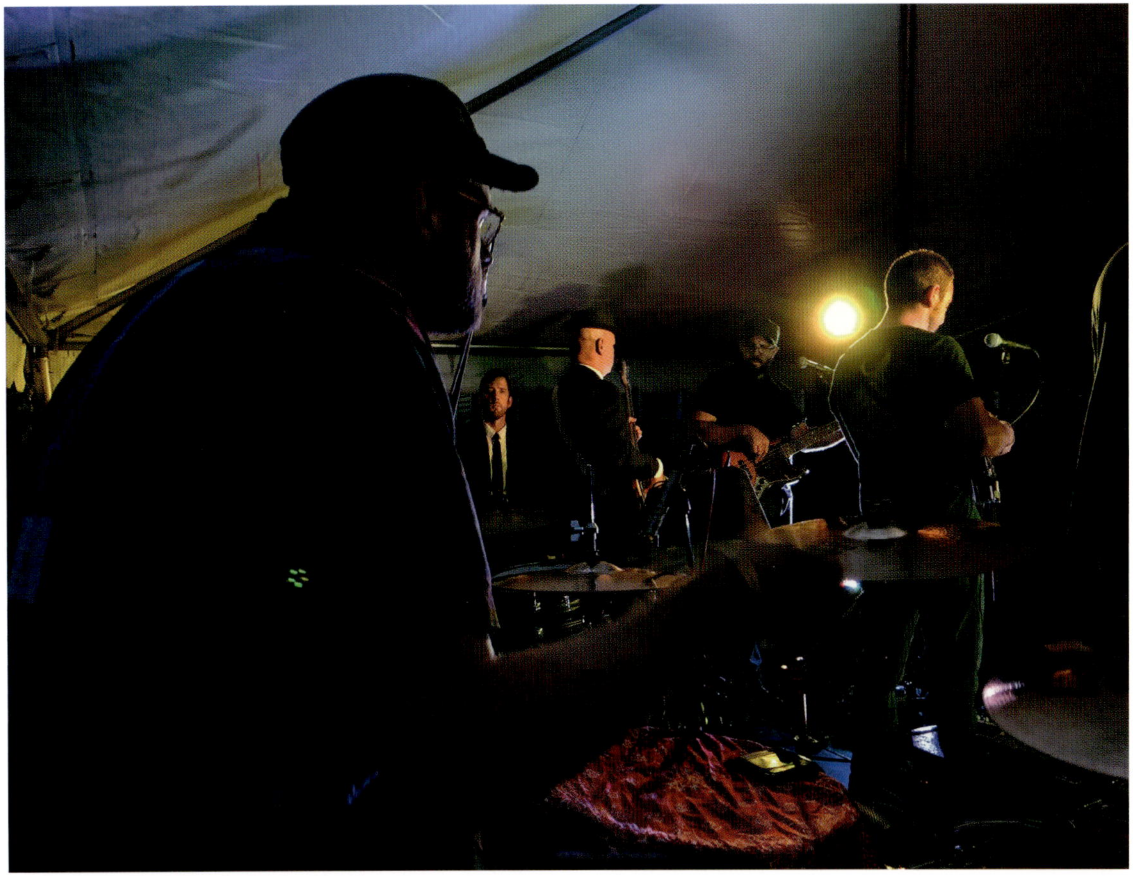

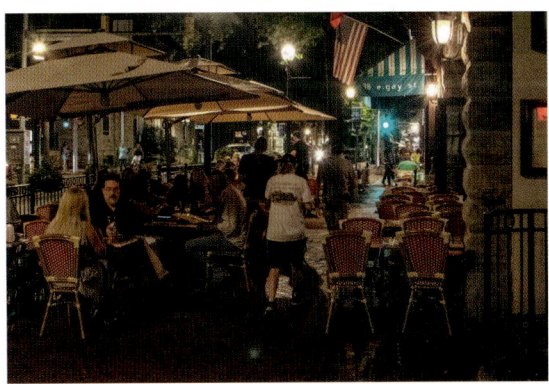
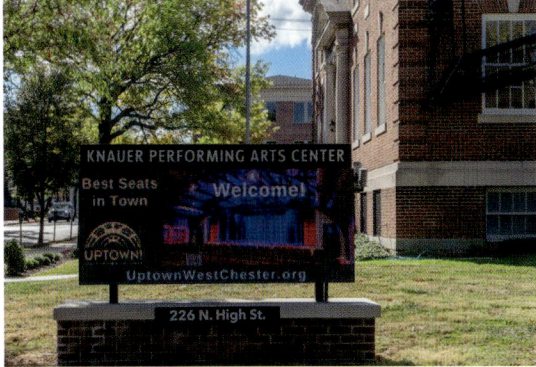

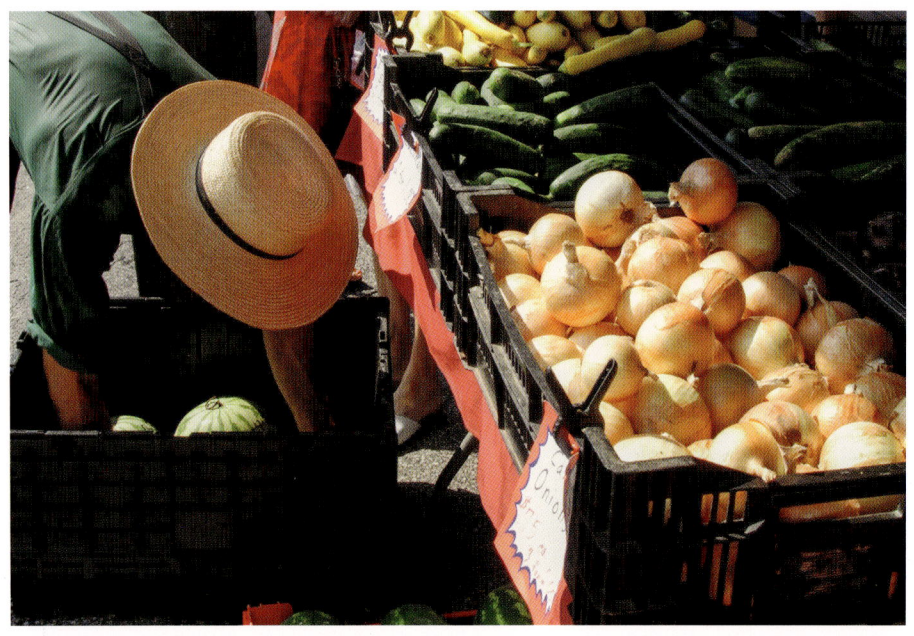

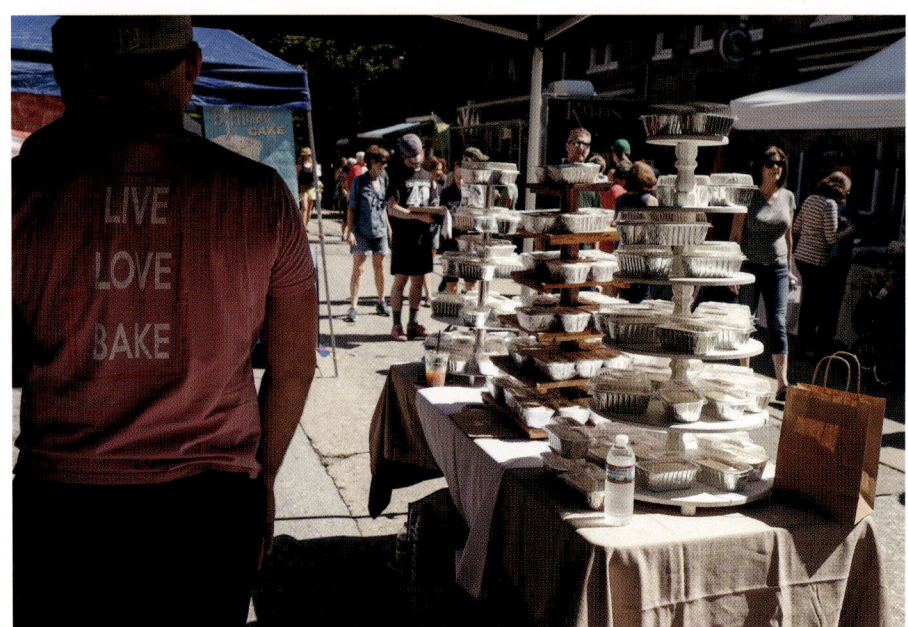

West Chester
West Chester Growers Market

West Chester
Restaurant Festival

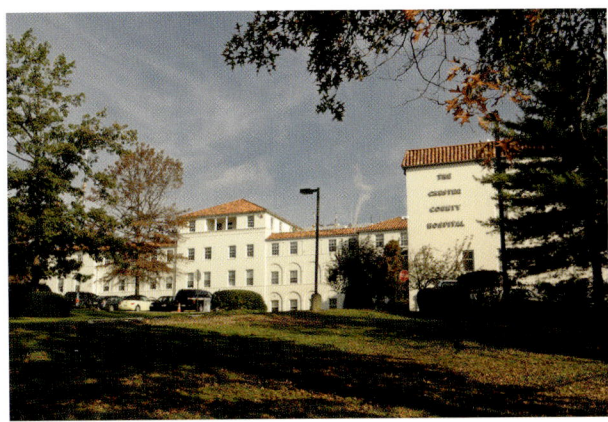

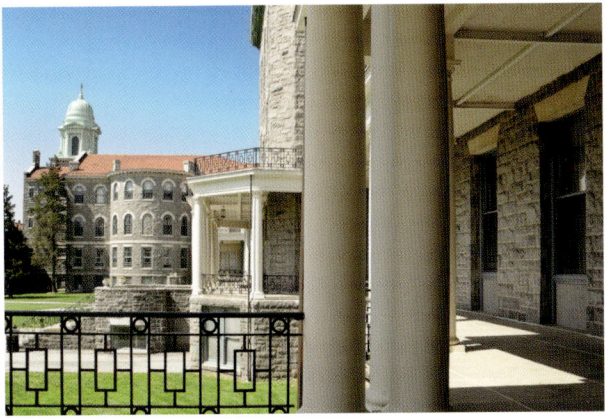

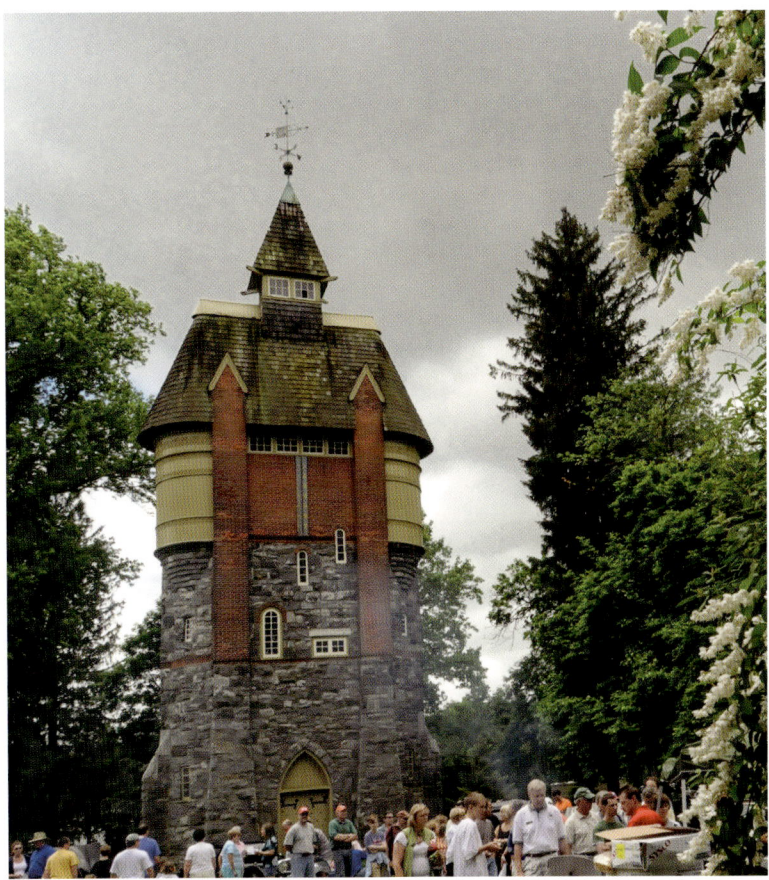

Chester County Hospital, West Chester
The county's first and leading hospital is part of the PennMedicine system.

Immaculata College, East Whiteland Township
The name Whiteland was brought by Welsh settlers from the Whiteland Gardens, in Flintshire, Wales. In contrast, Native Americans called the area the Dark Valley because of the numerous trees and undergrowth.

Westtown Township
Oakbourne Mansion's idiosyncratic water tower, Oakbourne Park

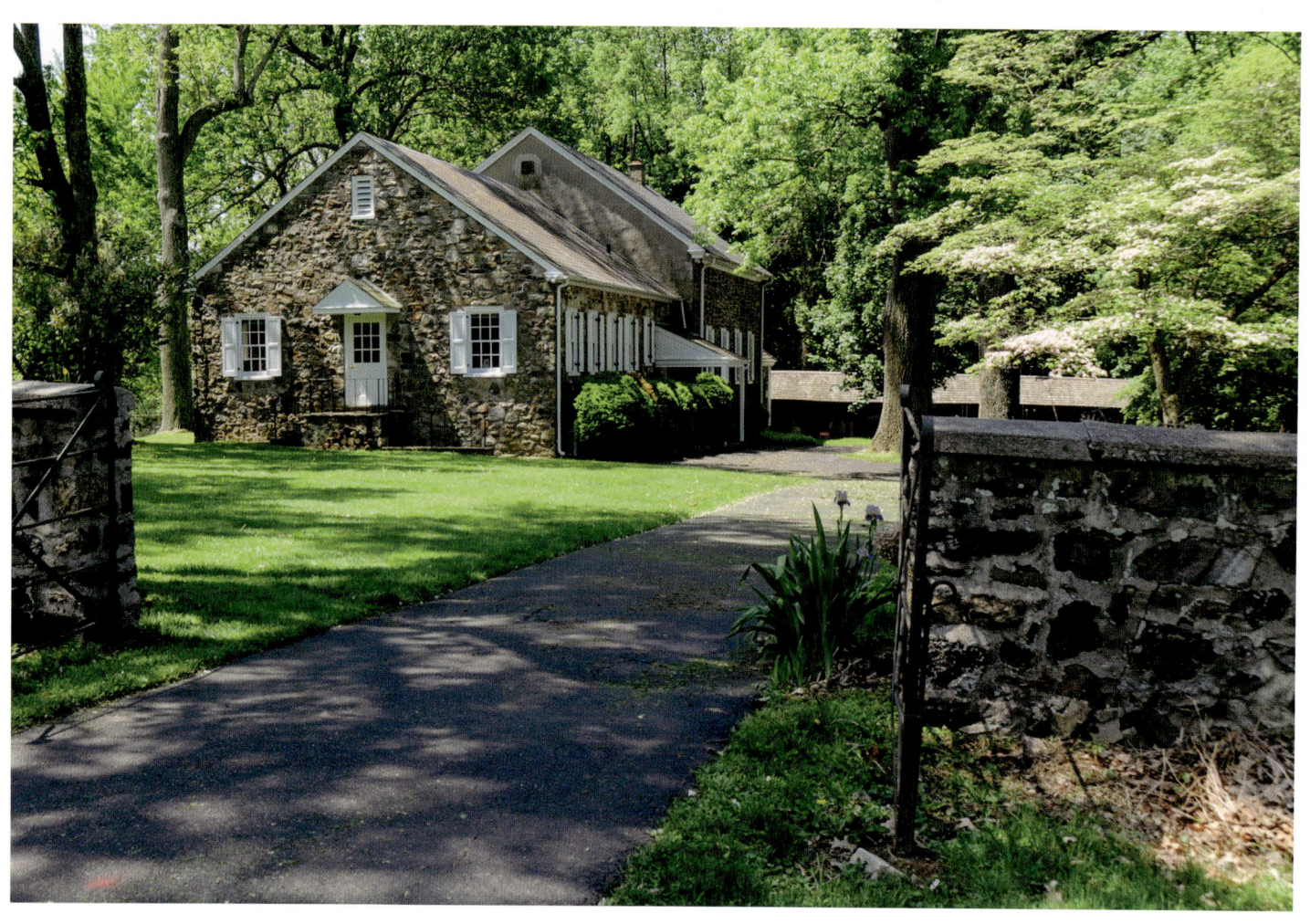

Willistown Township
Willistown Friends Meeting

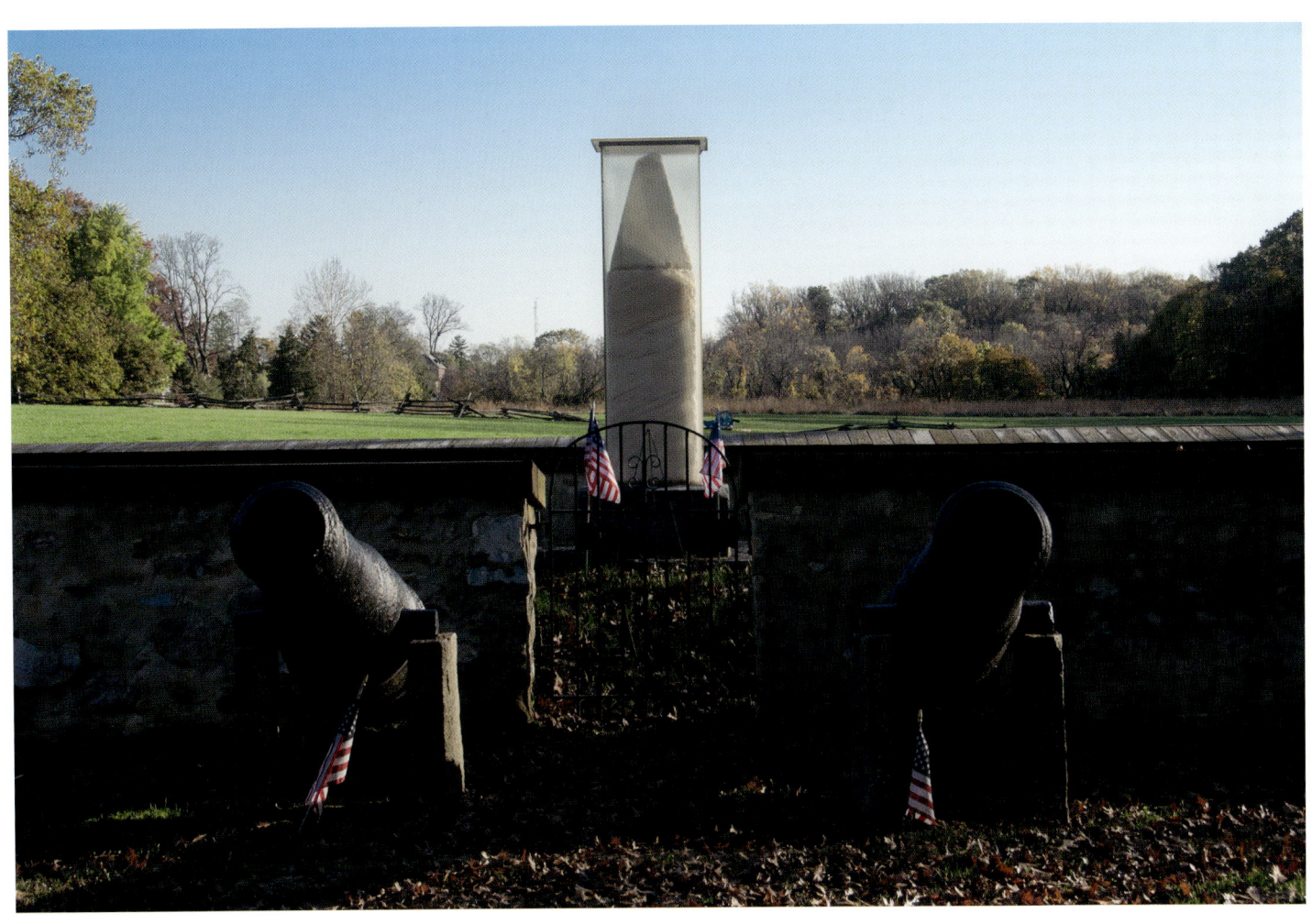

Malvern
Paoli Massacre Memorial

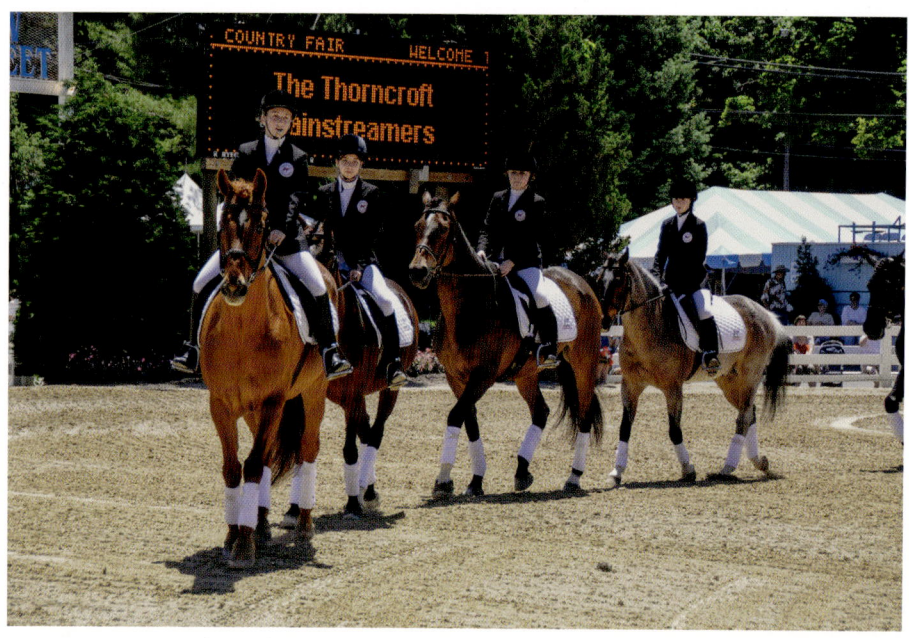

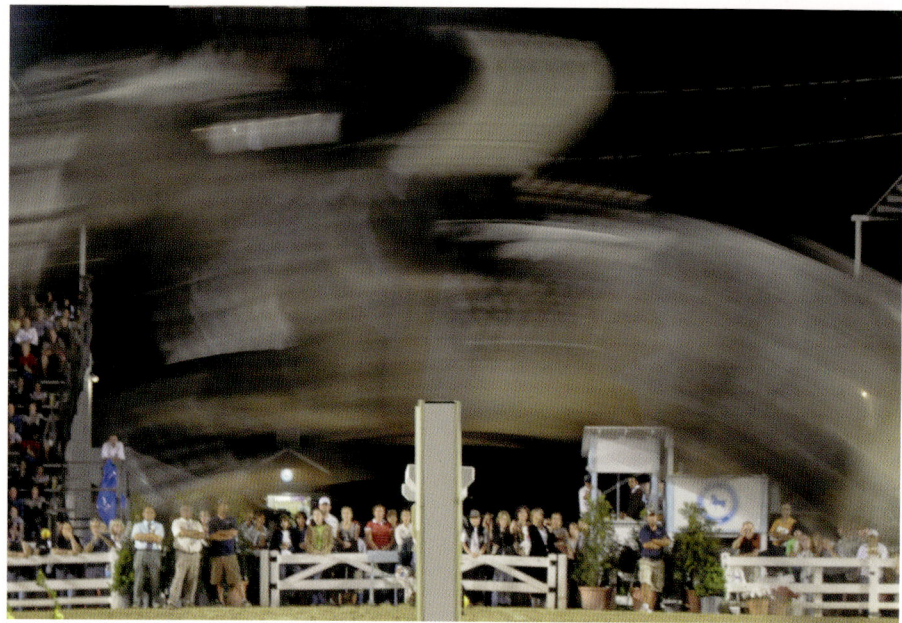

Devon
Devon Horse Show

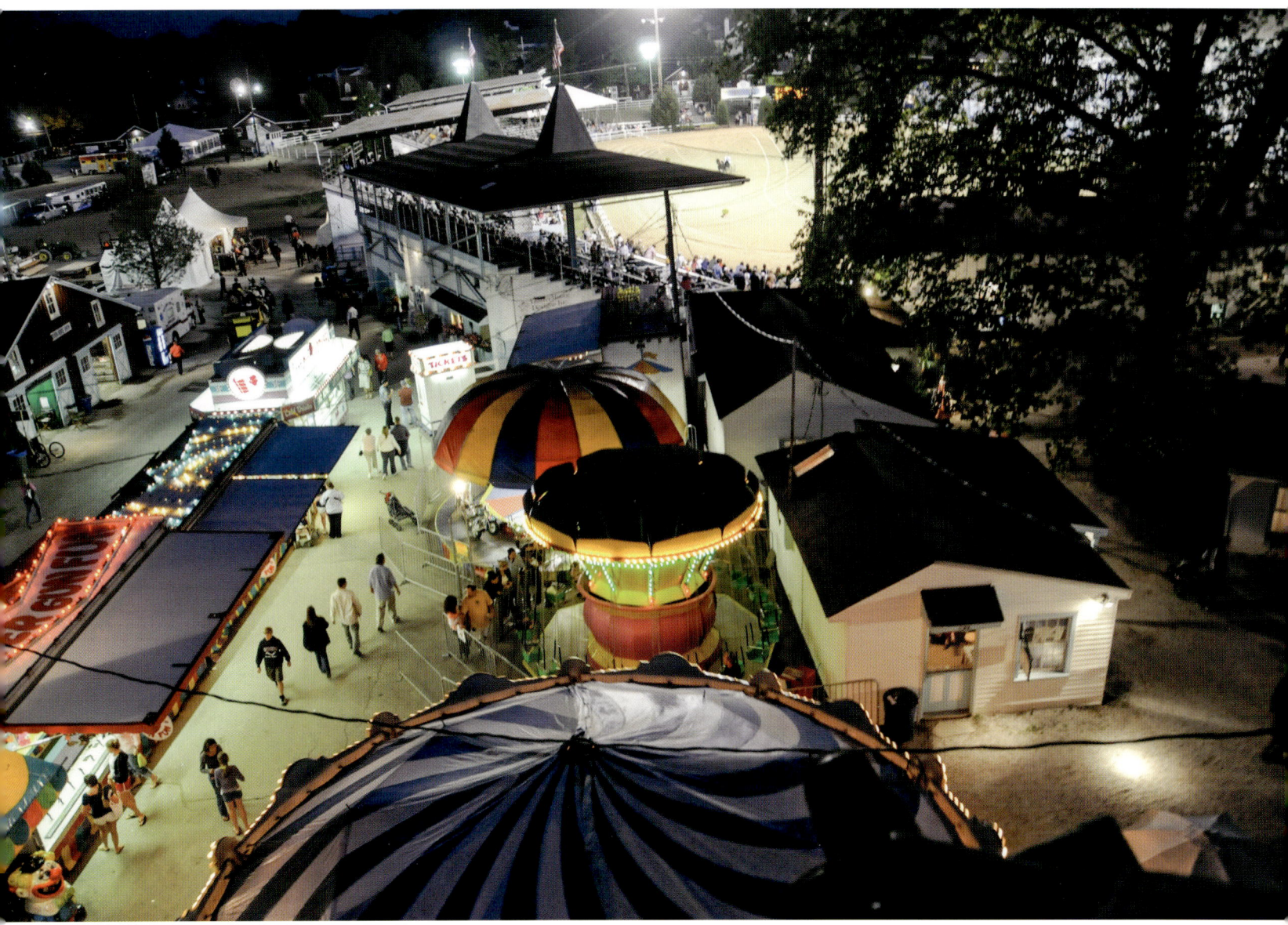

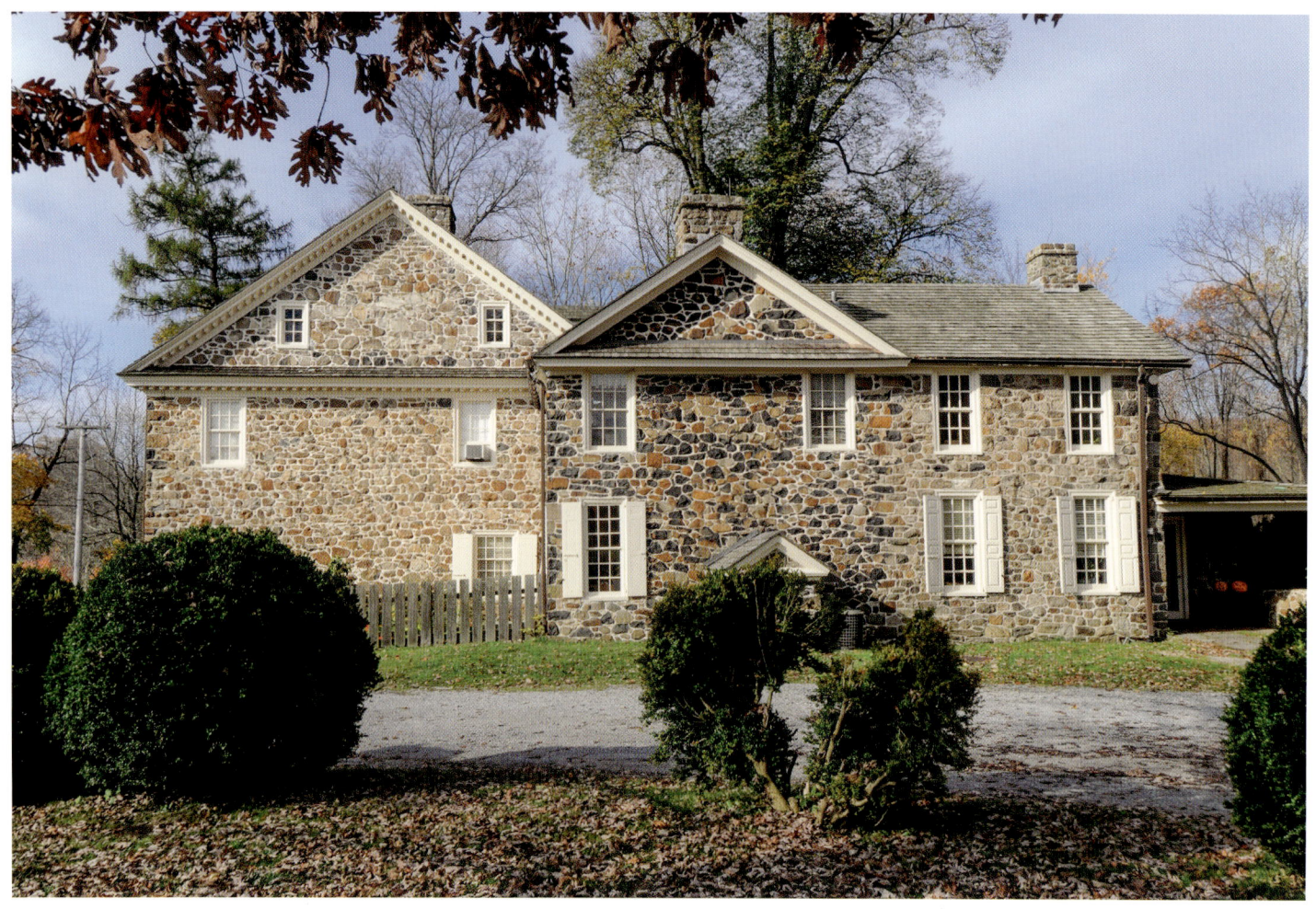

Easttown Township
Historic Waynesborough, homestead of General Anthony Wayne

Easttown Township
Historic St. David's Church

Lafayette Birmingham Cemetery, Birmingham Township
The township was named by settlers from Birmingham, England, and organized in 1686. Many of those killed during the Battle of the Brandywine are buried here.

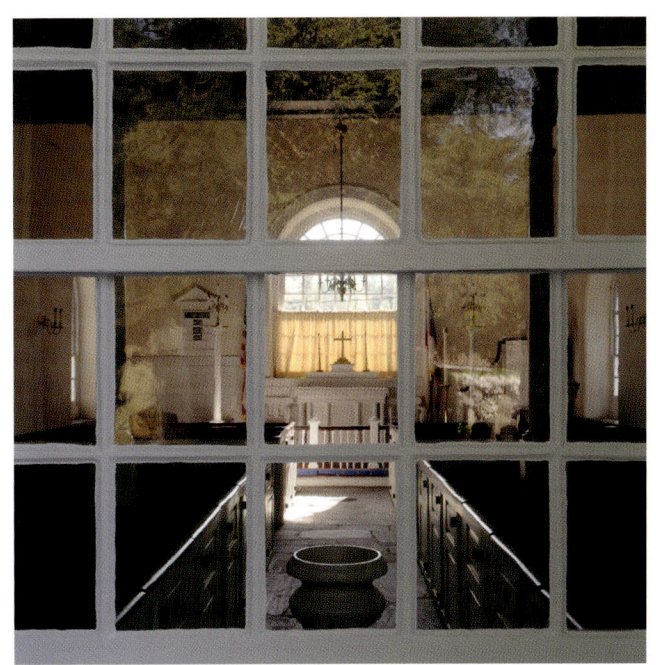
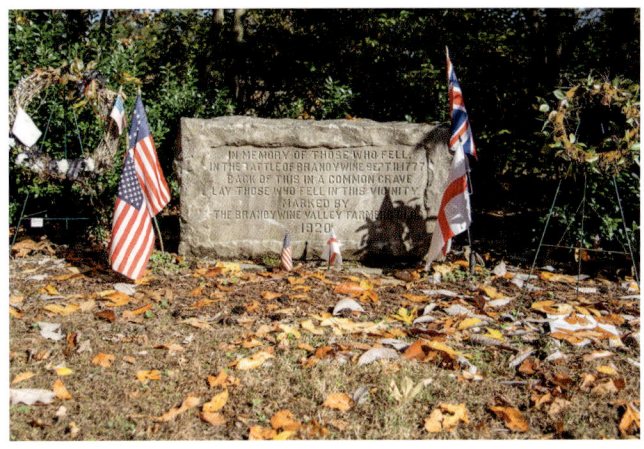
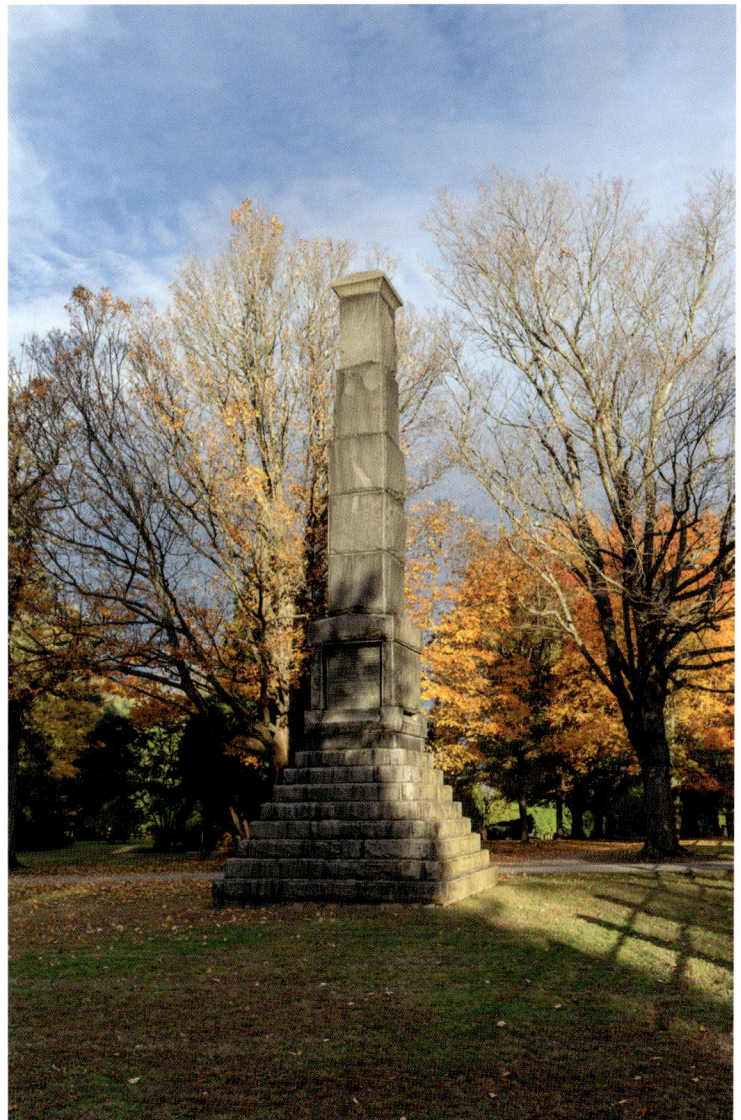

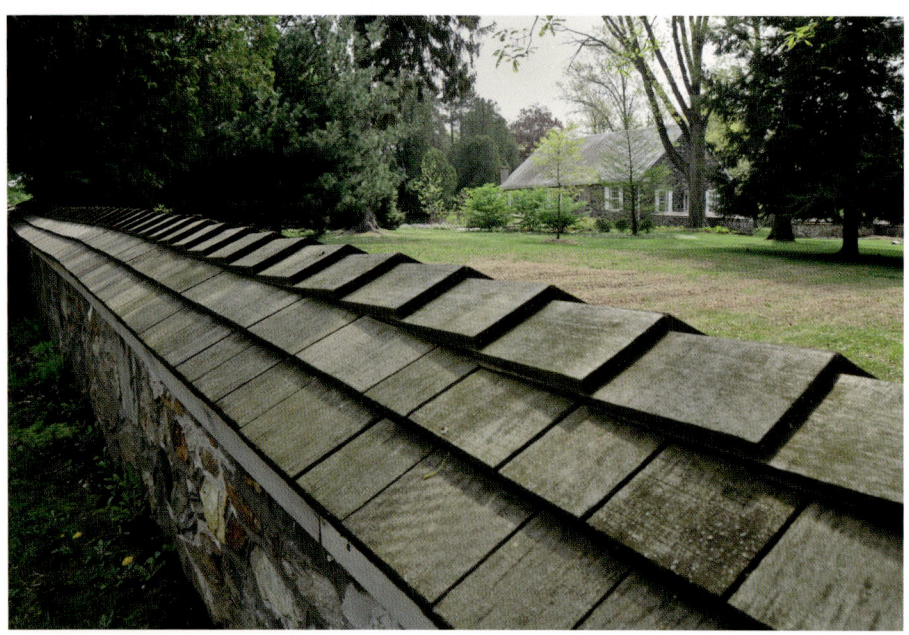

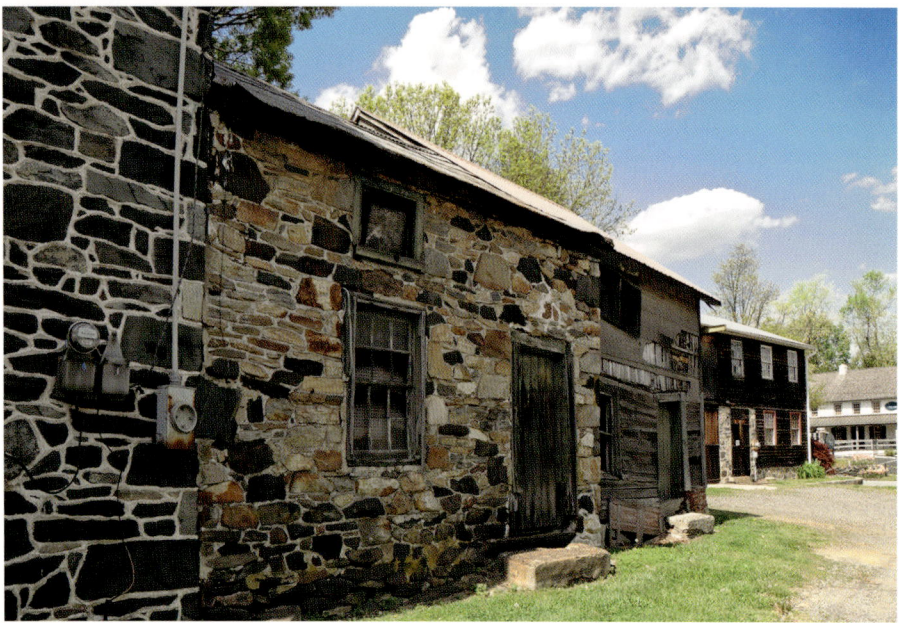

Birmingham Township
The Birmingham Friends Meeting House was used as a hospital during the Battle of Brandywine in 1777, as was the nearby Dilworthtown Inn.

Dilworthtown, Birmingham Township
Dilworthtown is on the National Register of Historic Places. During the American Revolution, it was the scene of the most vigorous fighting of the Battle of Brandywine, September 11, 1777. Dilworthtown was severely damaged by marauding British troops.

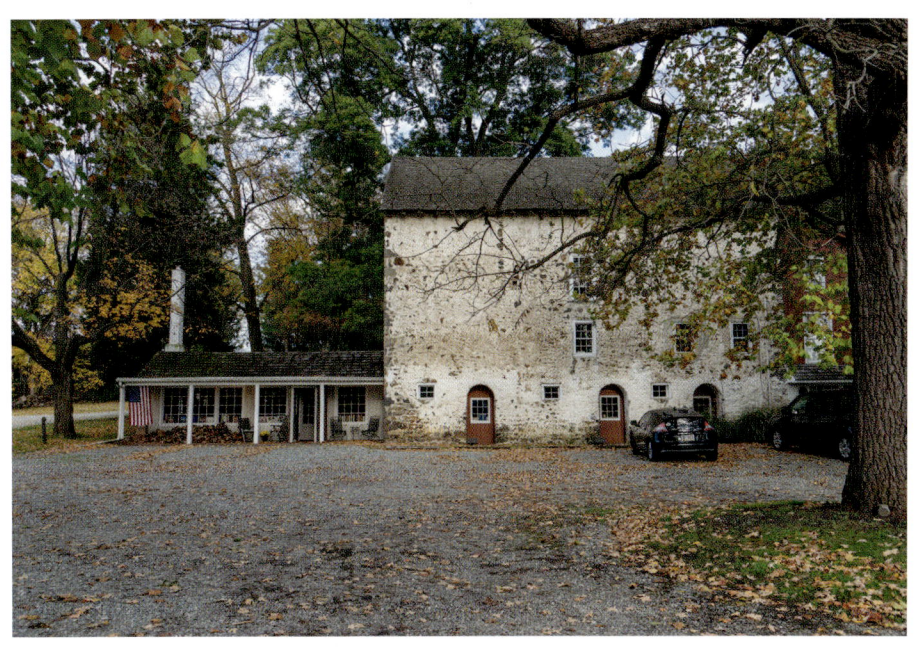

East Bradford Township
Baldwin's Book Barn is a former barn turned into a sprawling store for used books.

East Fallowfield Township
Hayes Clark Covered Bridge, the Laurels Preserve

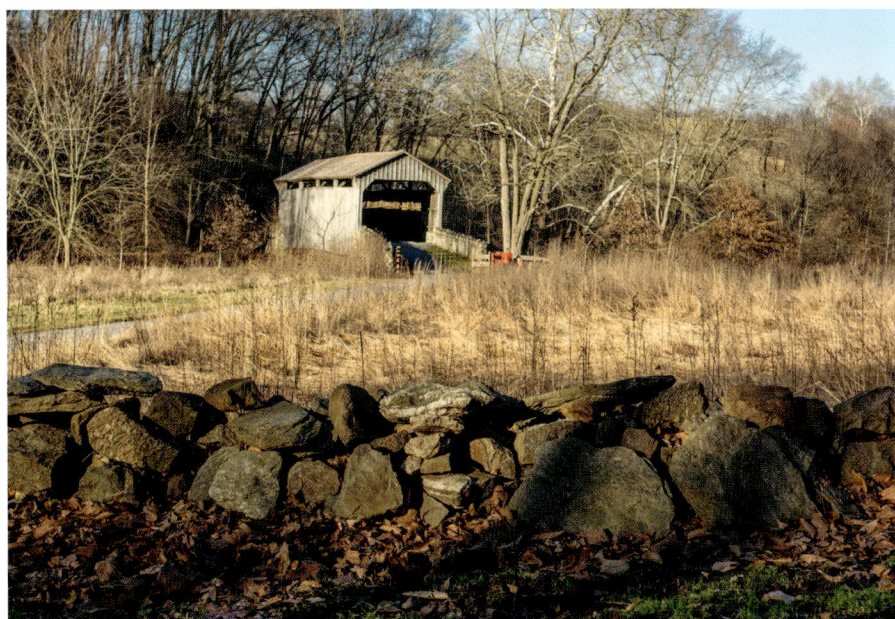

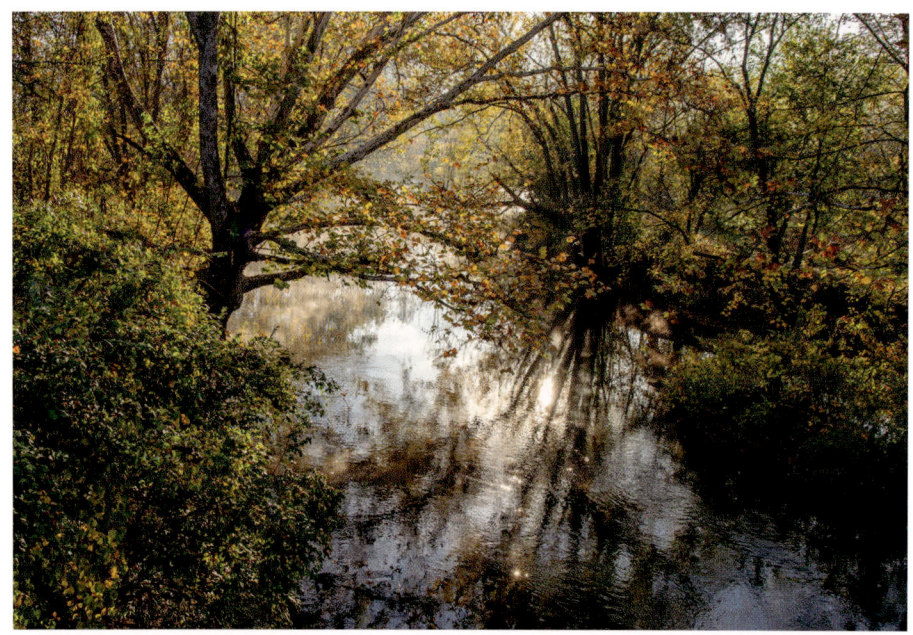

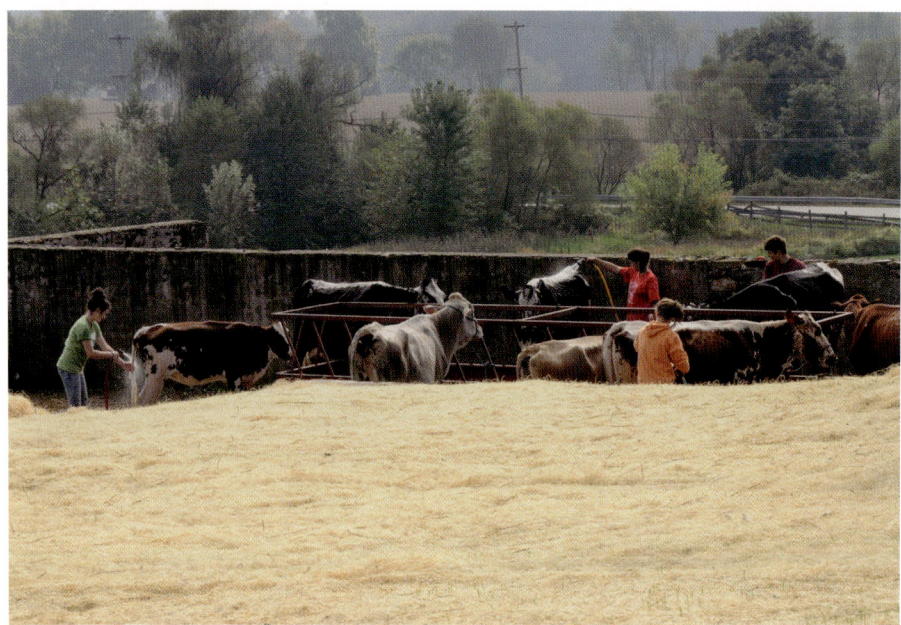

East Fallowfield Township
Brandywine Creek, the Laurels Preserve

East Marlborough Township
Unionville Community Fair

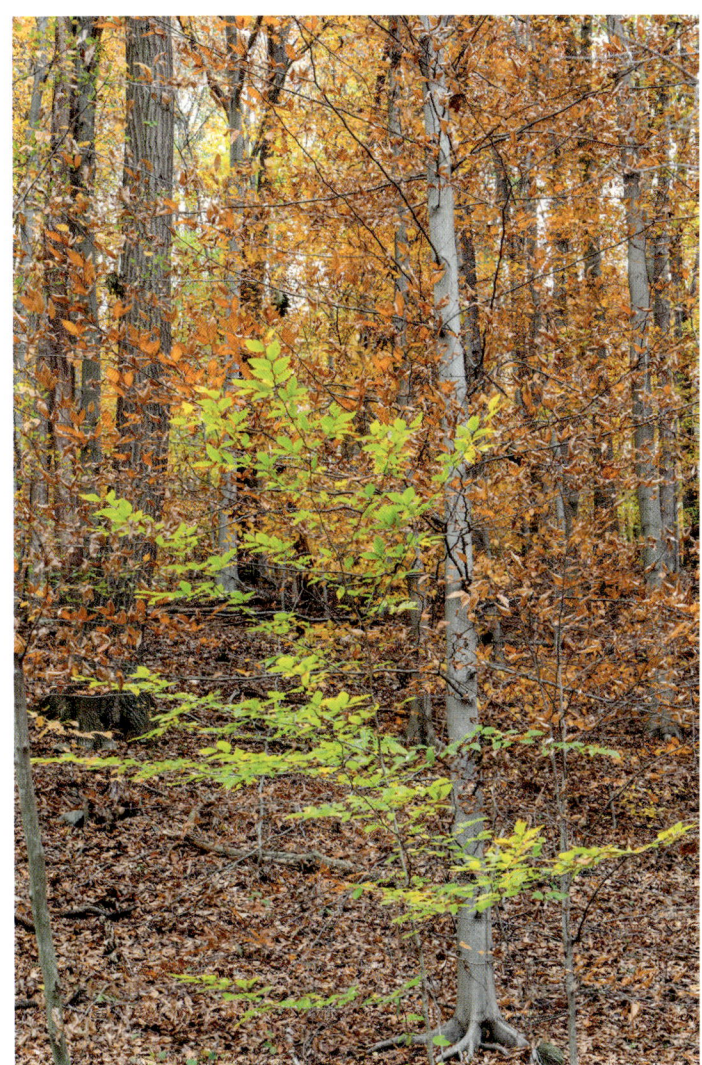 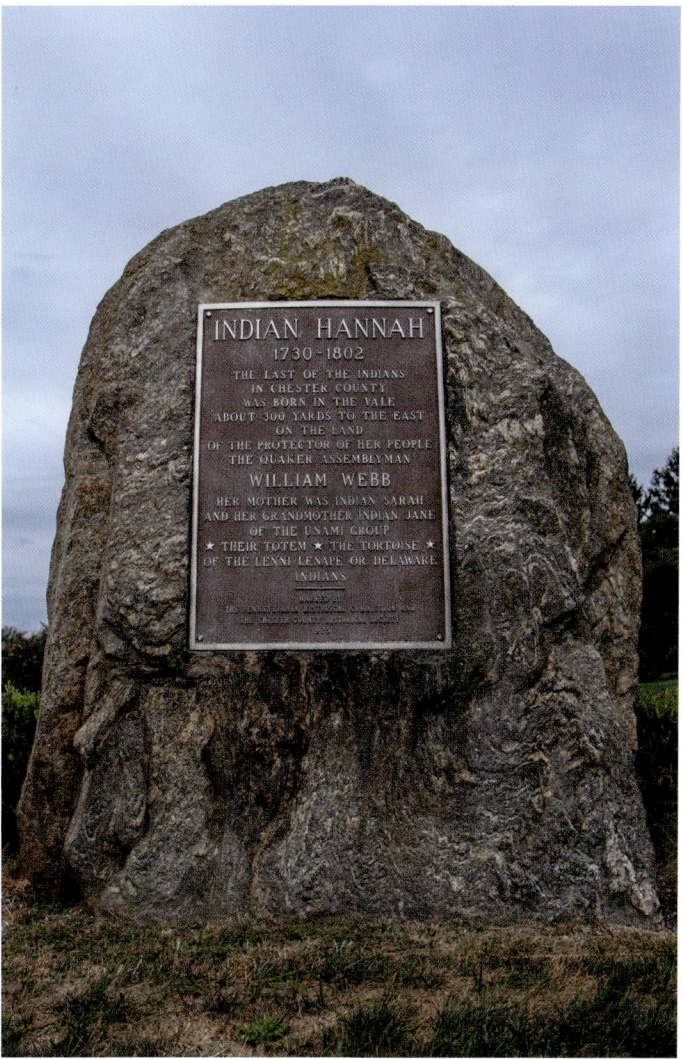

East Fallowfield Township
The Laurels Preserve

Kennett Township
Monument commemorating Indian Hannah, the last
Lenni Lenape Native American to live in the area

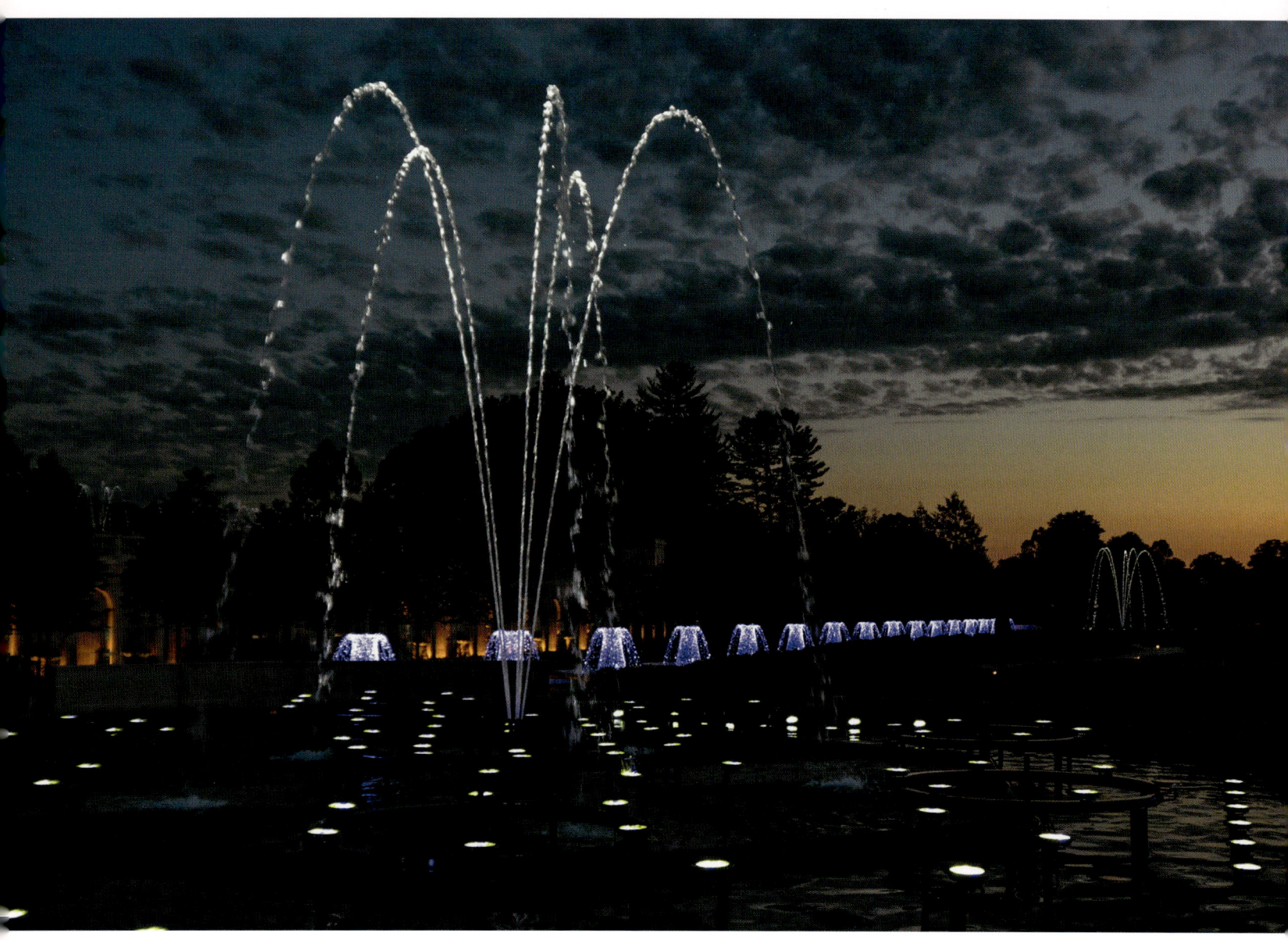

East Marlborough Township
Longwood Gardens

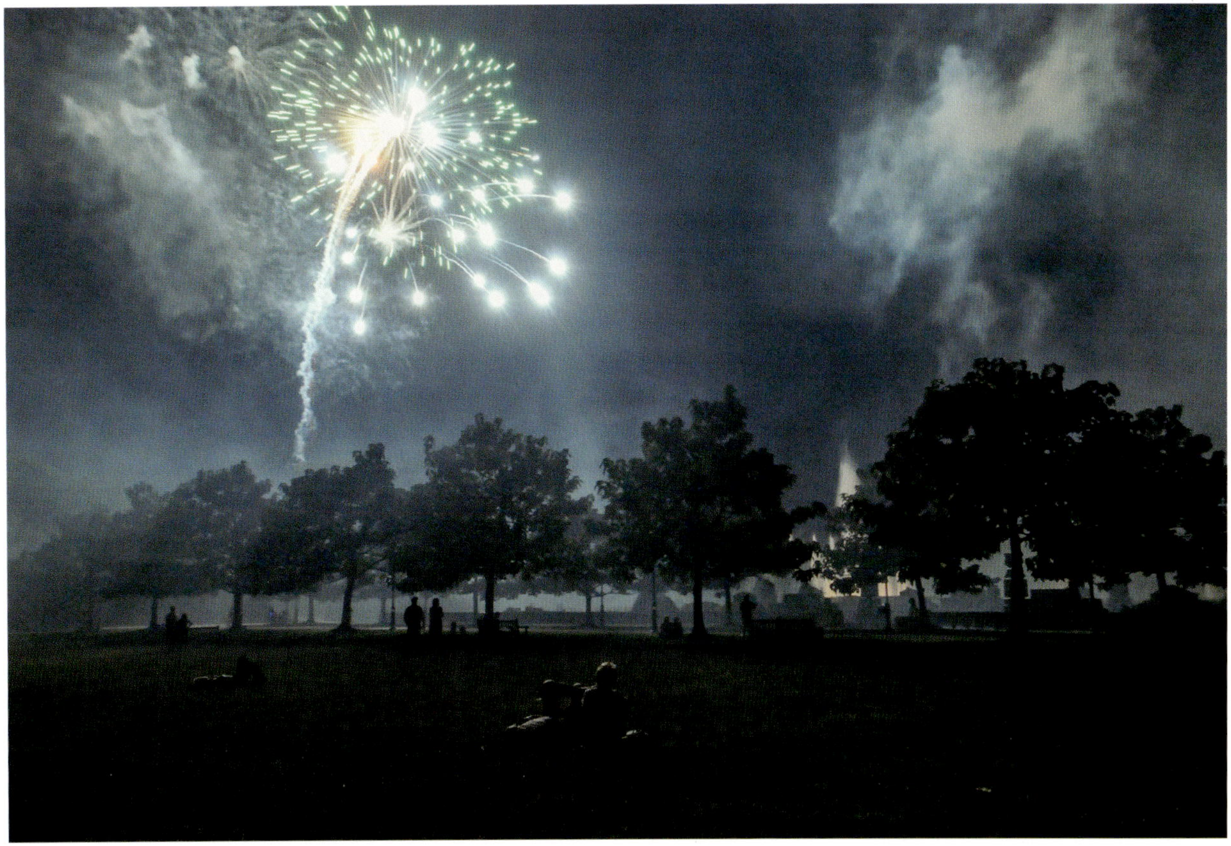

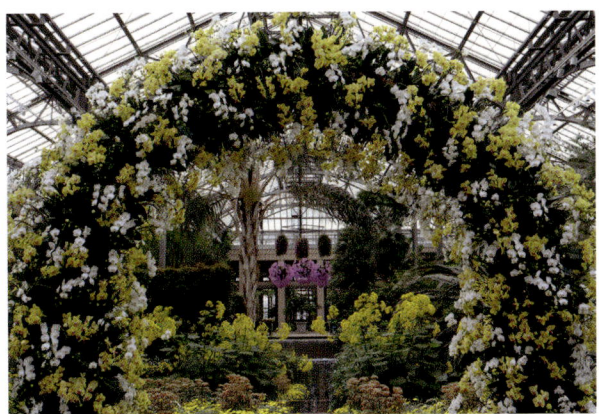
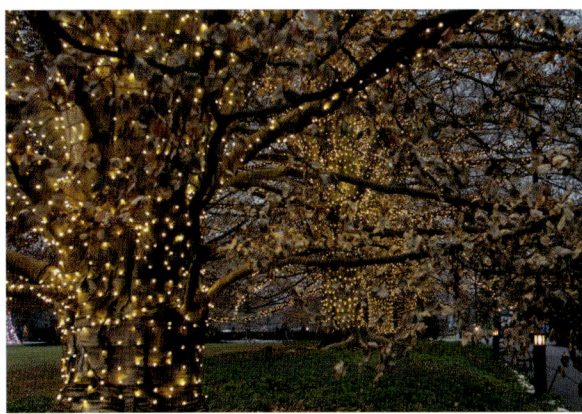

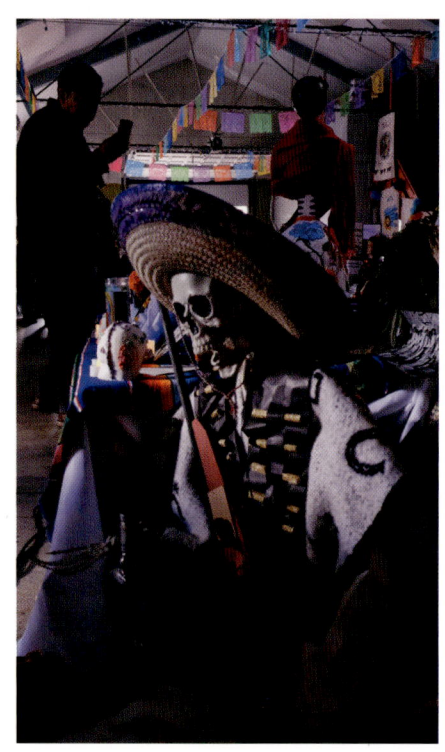 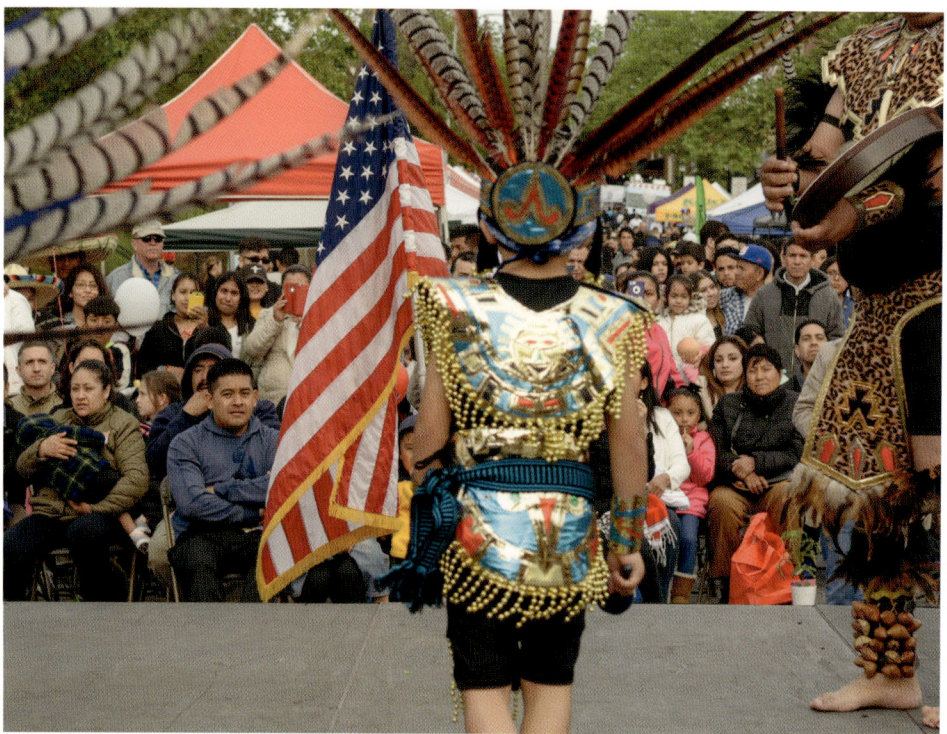

Kennett Square
Día de los Muertos celebration

Kennett Square
Annual Cinco de Mayo celebration

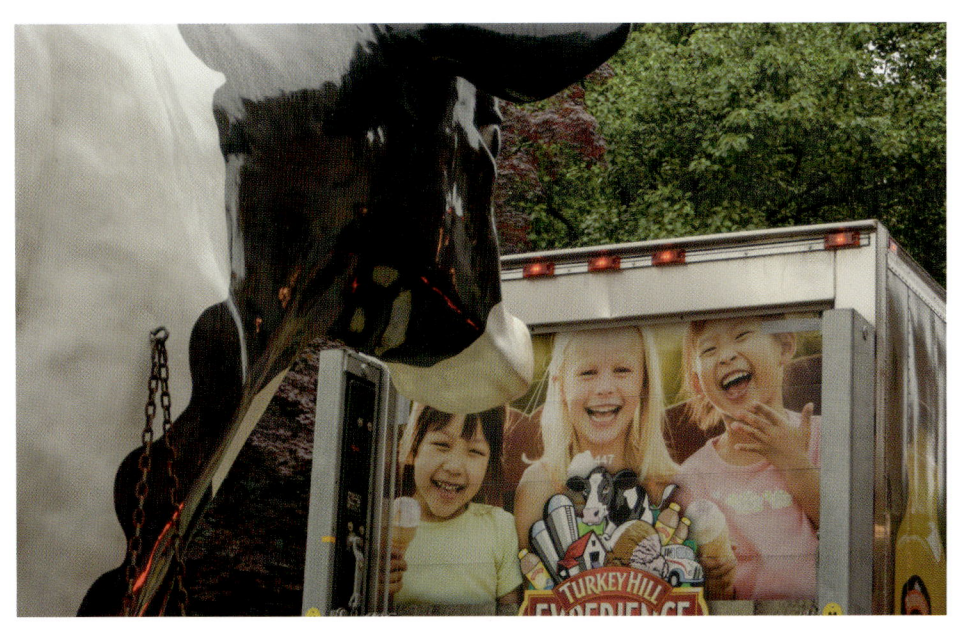

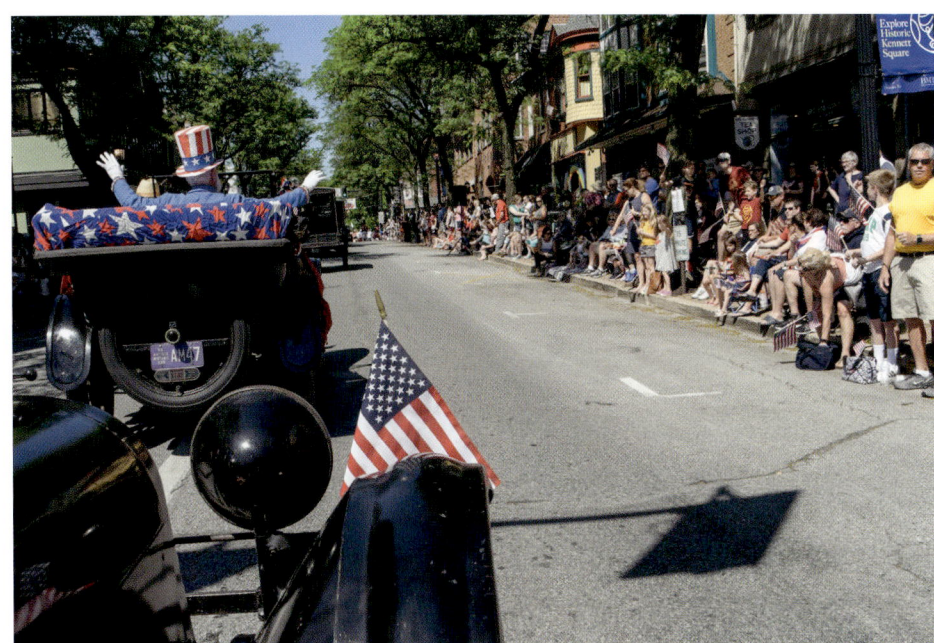

Memorial Day Parade, Kennett Square
The town was originally called "Kennet" after a village in Wiltshire, England, from where one of the founders, Francis Smith, hailed.

Kennett Square
Many prominent citizens in and around the town helped slaves escape via the Underground Railroad.

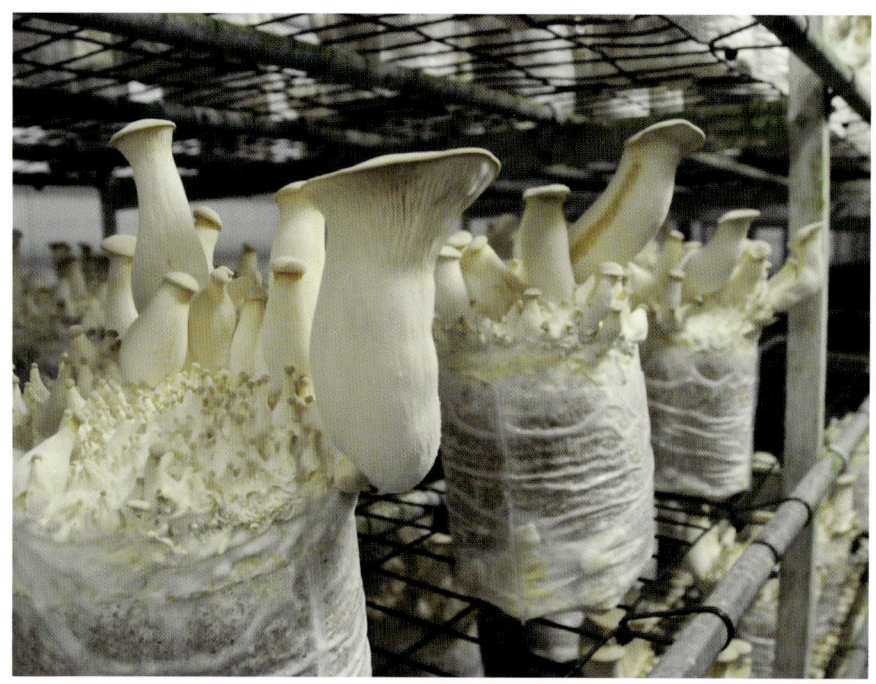

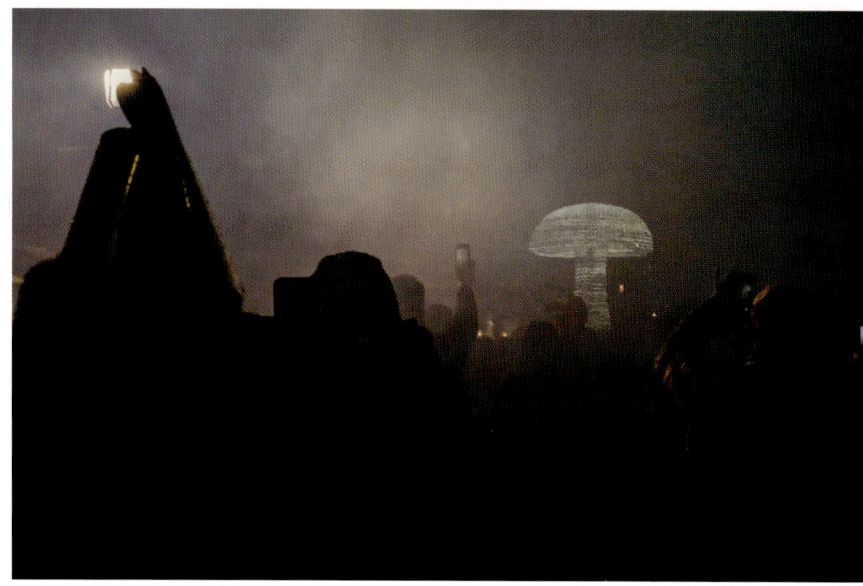

Kennett Square
Royal Trumpet mushrooms at Phillips Mushroom Farms, the largest grower of specialty mushrooms in the US

Kennett Square
The mushroom drops on New Year's Eve.

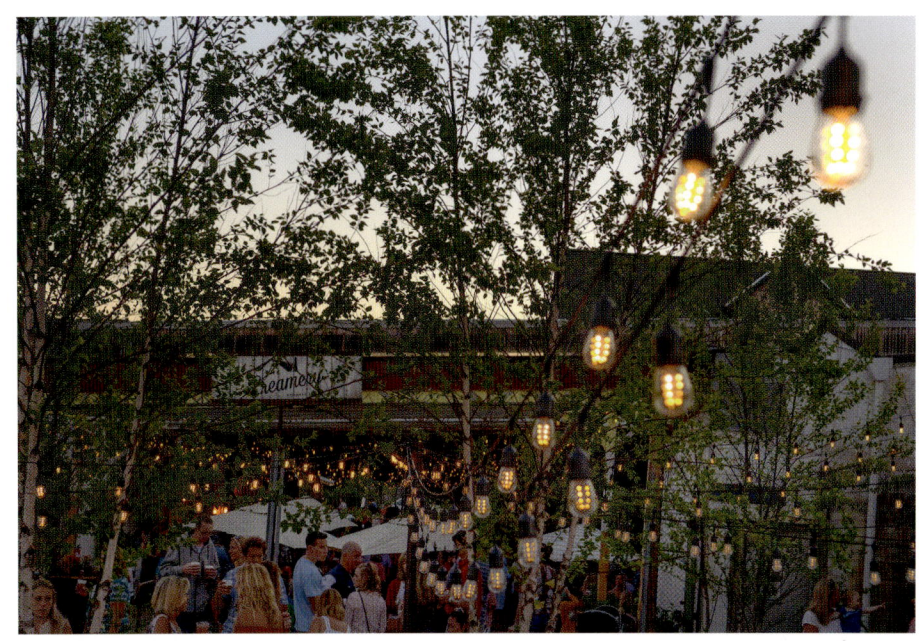

Kennett Square
The Creamery

Kennett Square
"The mushroom capital of the world." William Swayne is credited with introducing mushroom growing to the area. Around 1885 he wanted to use the wasted space under elevated beds, so he imported spawn from Europe and experimented with mushroom cultivation.

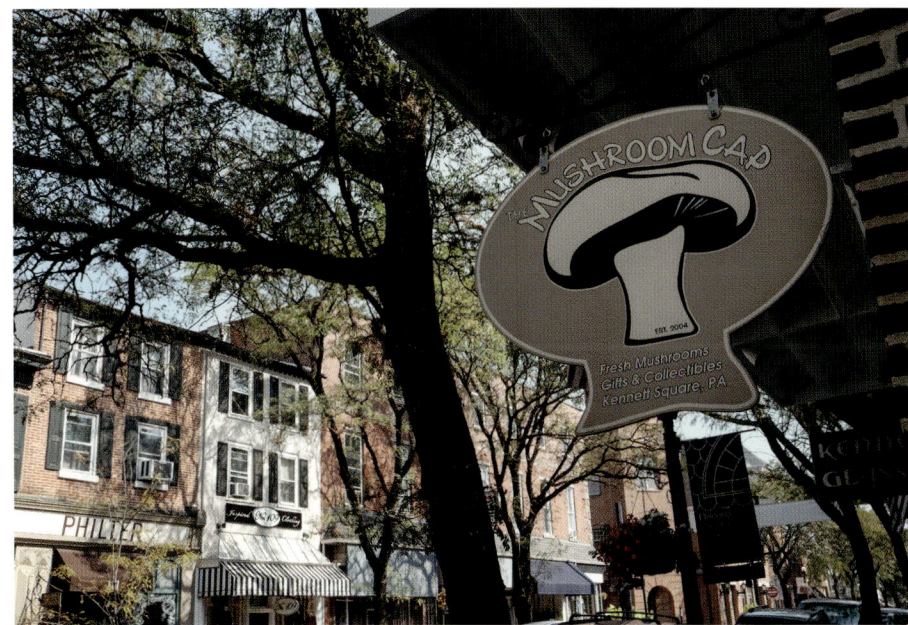

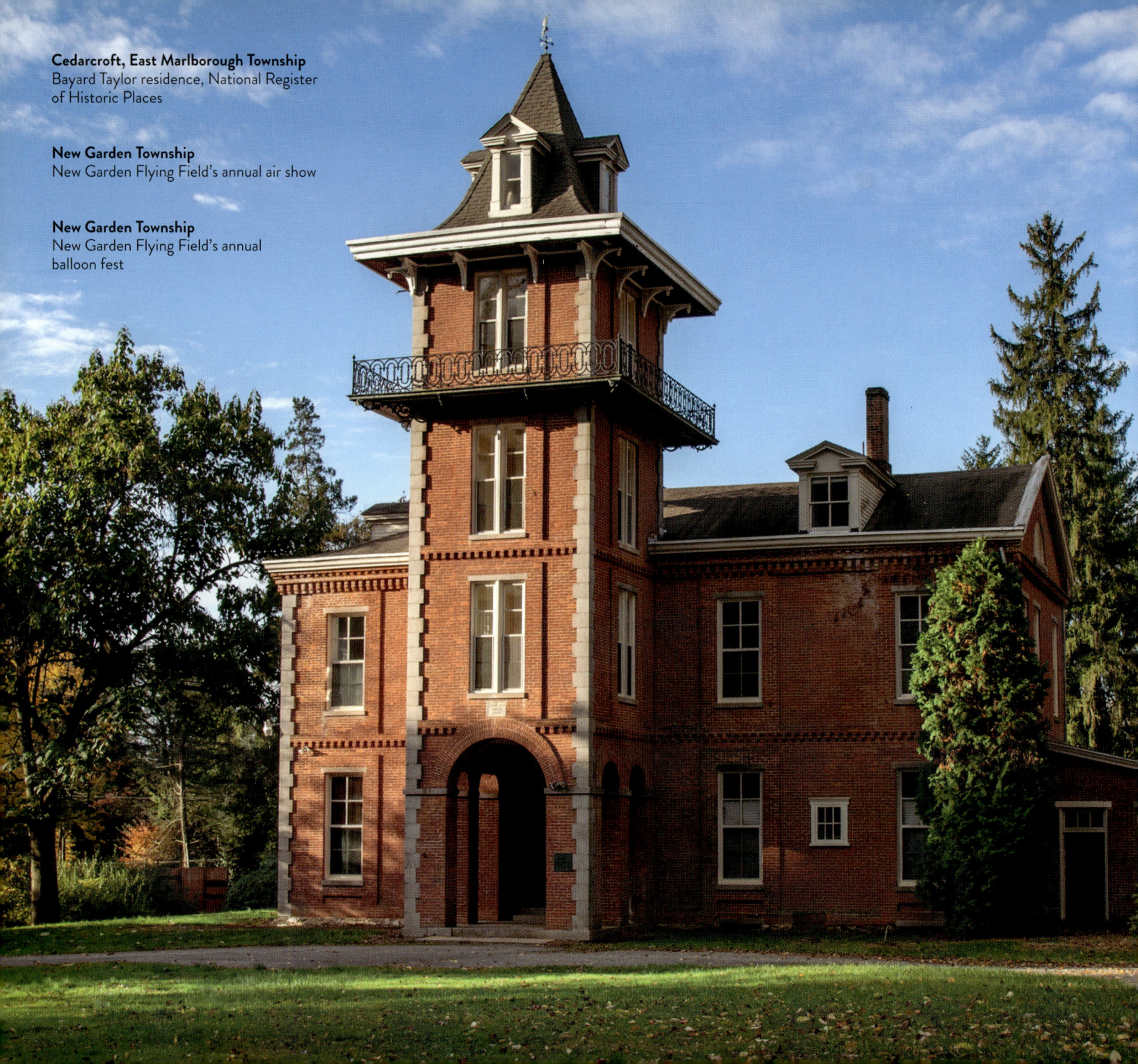

Cedarcroft, East Marlborough Township
Bayard Taylor residence, National Register of Historic Places

New Garden Township
New Garden Flying Field's annual air show

New Garden Township
New Garden Flying Field's annual balloon fest

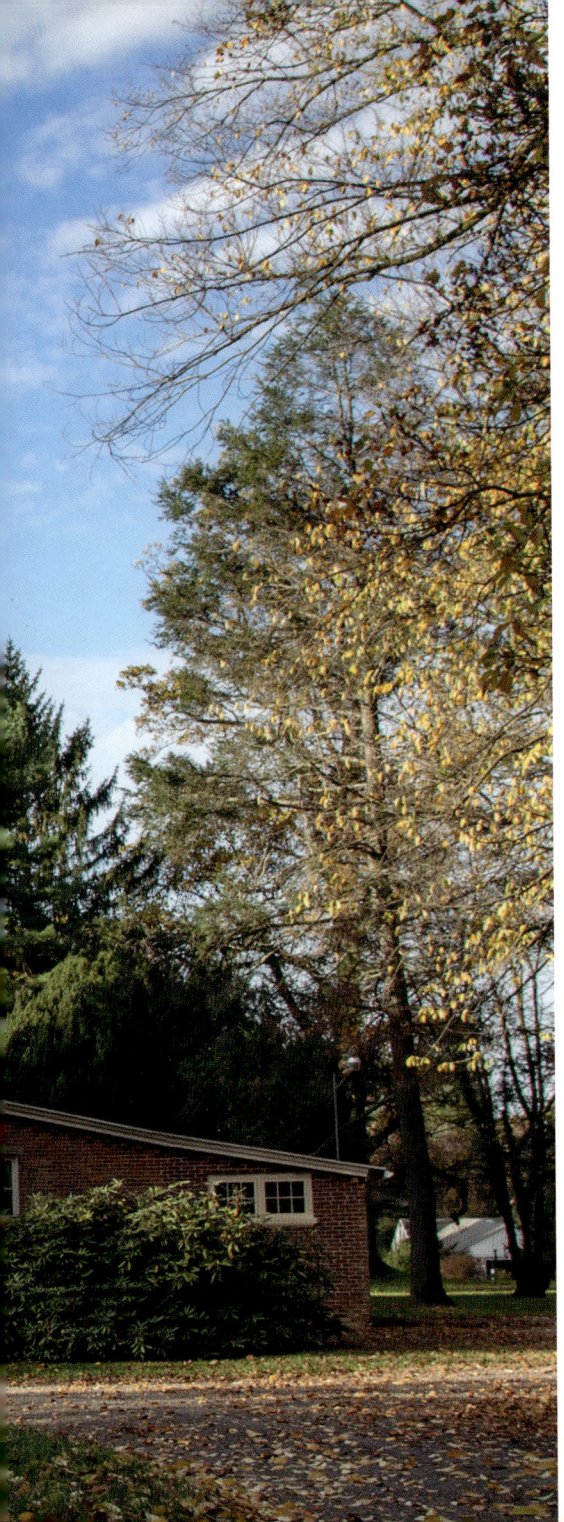
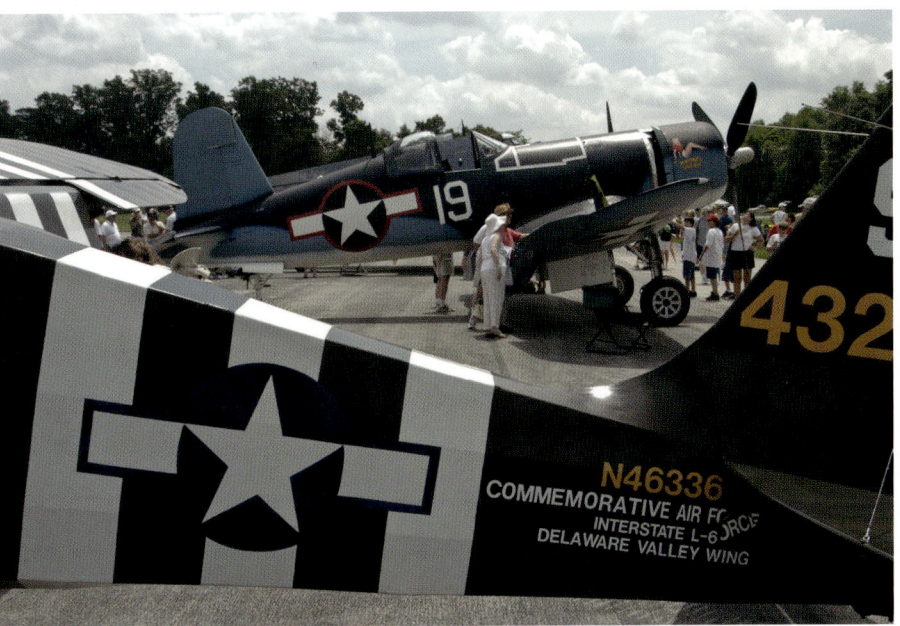
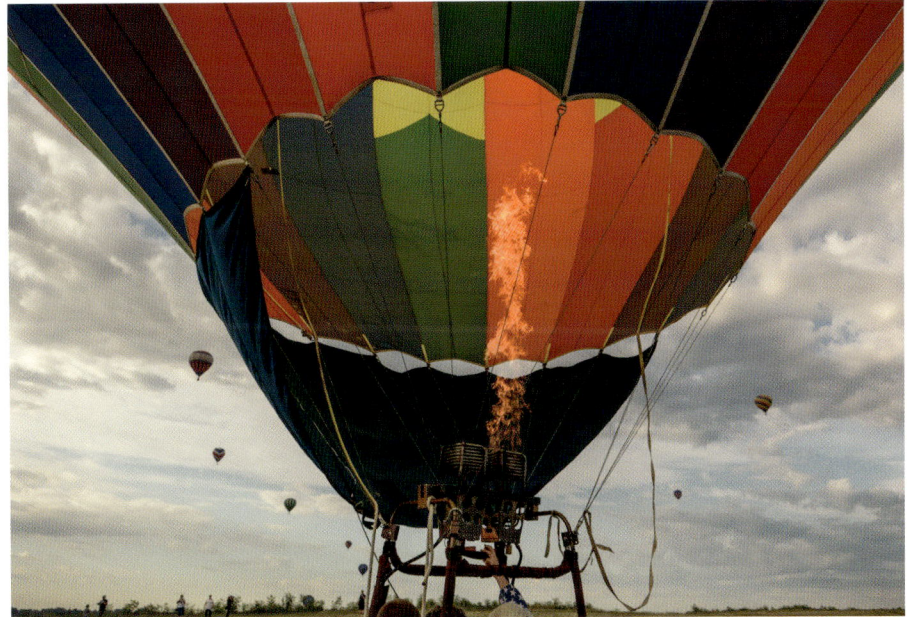

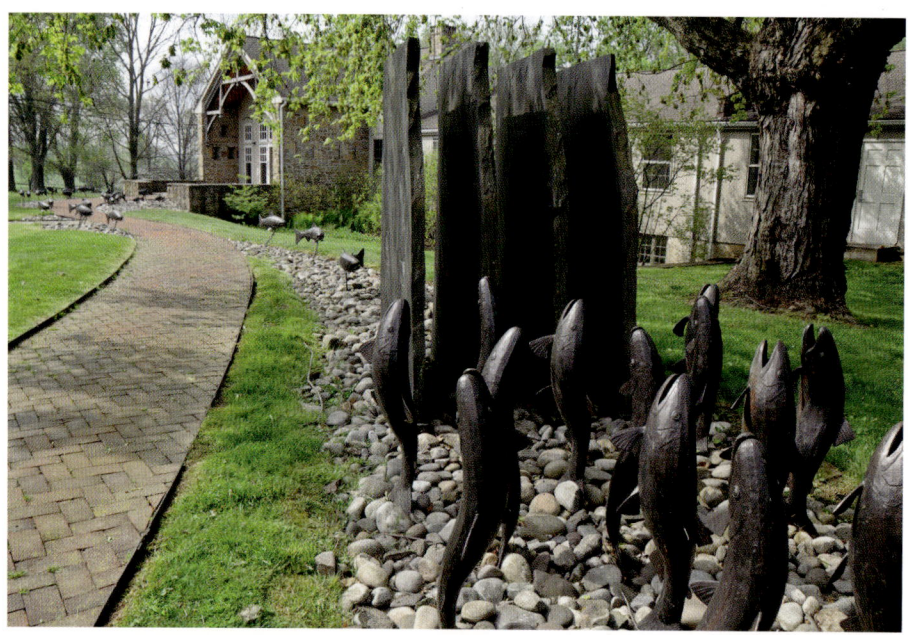

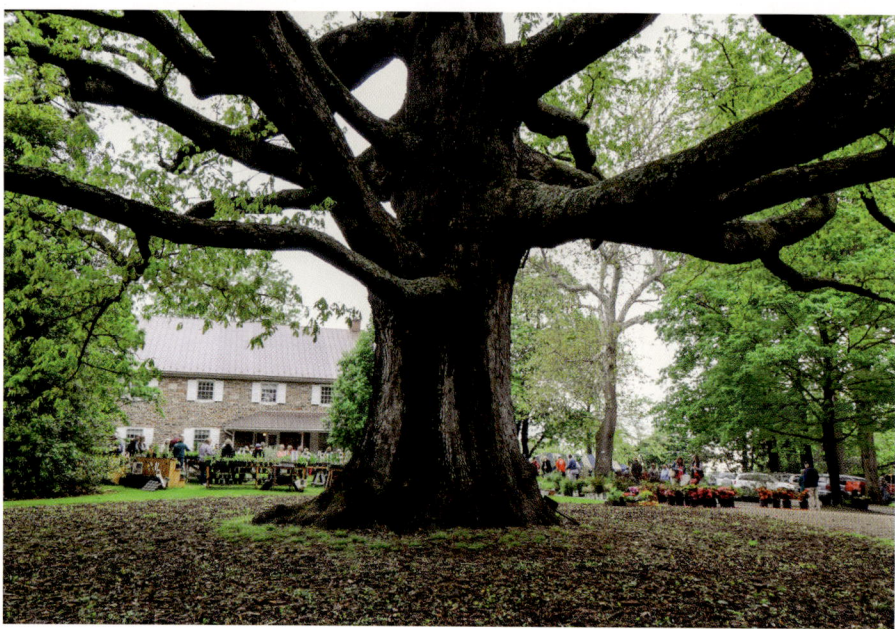

London Grove Township
Stroud Water Research Center, a world-class organization devoted to the study of streams and rivers nationally and internationally

London Grove Meeting House, West Marlborough Township
A plaque on this white oak tree reads: "This tree was living when William Penn came to Pennsylvania in 1682." The "Penn oak tree" is over 335 years old and still going strong.

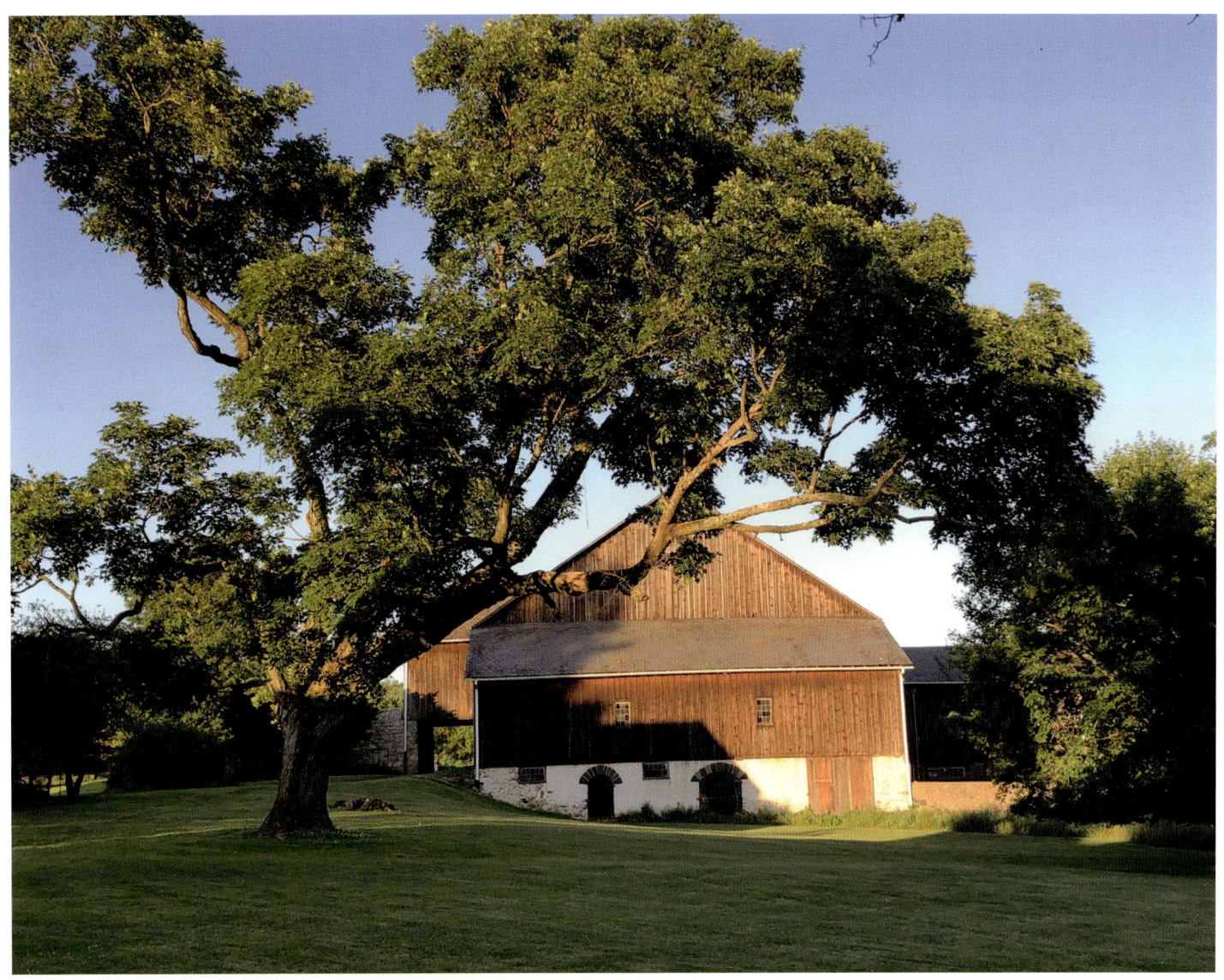

East Marlboro Township
Scarlet Thicket Farm, site of the annual Scarlet Thicket Art Show

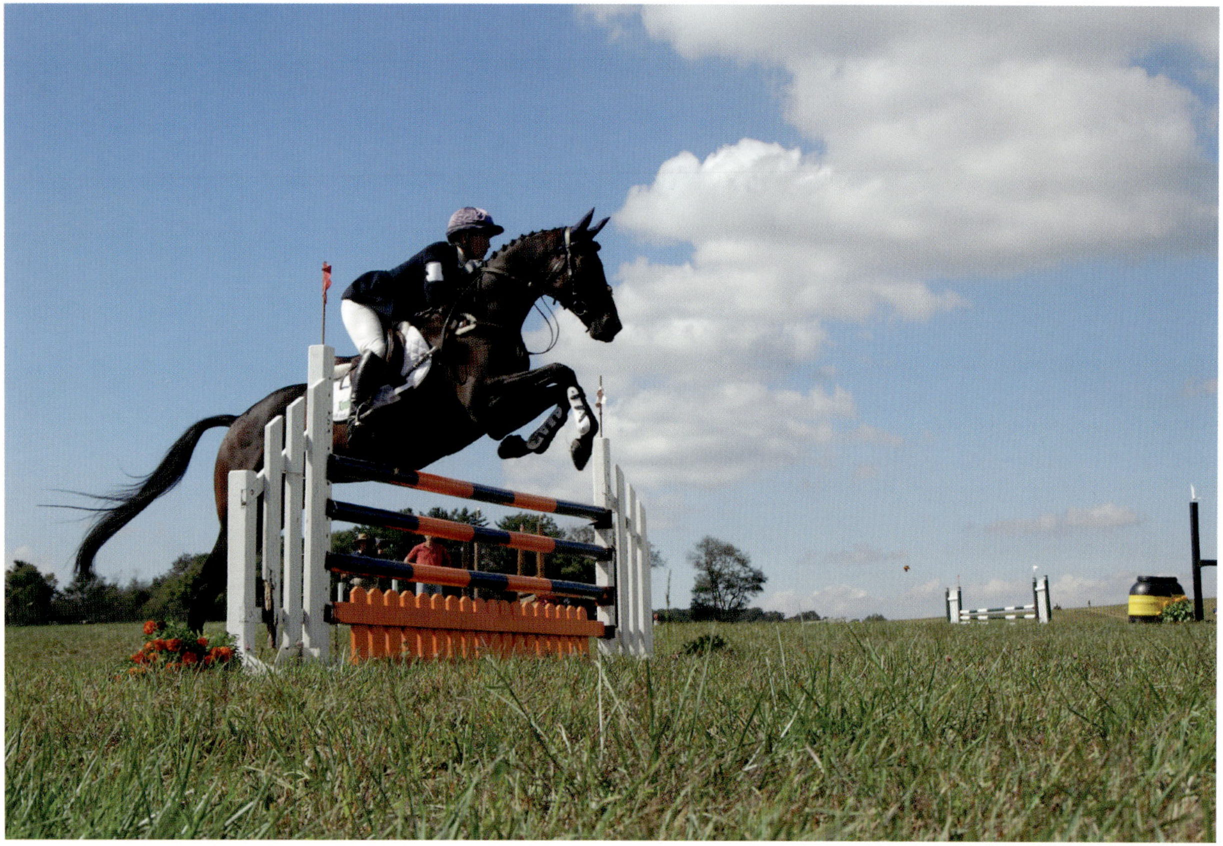

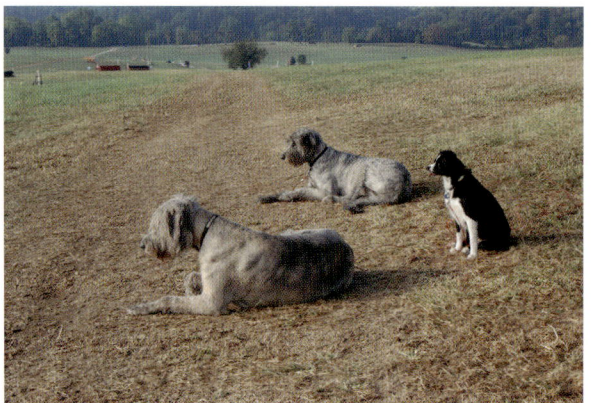
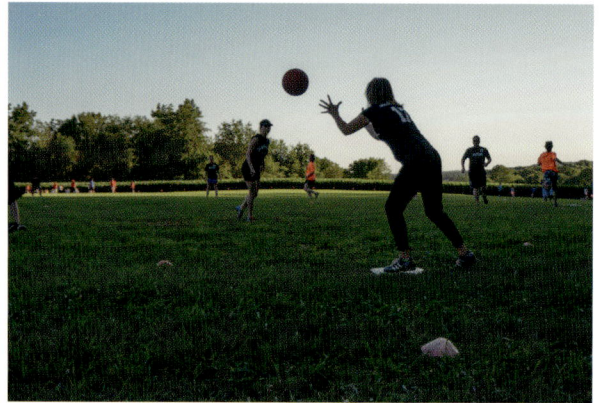

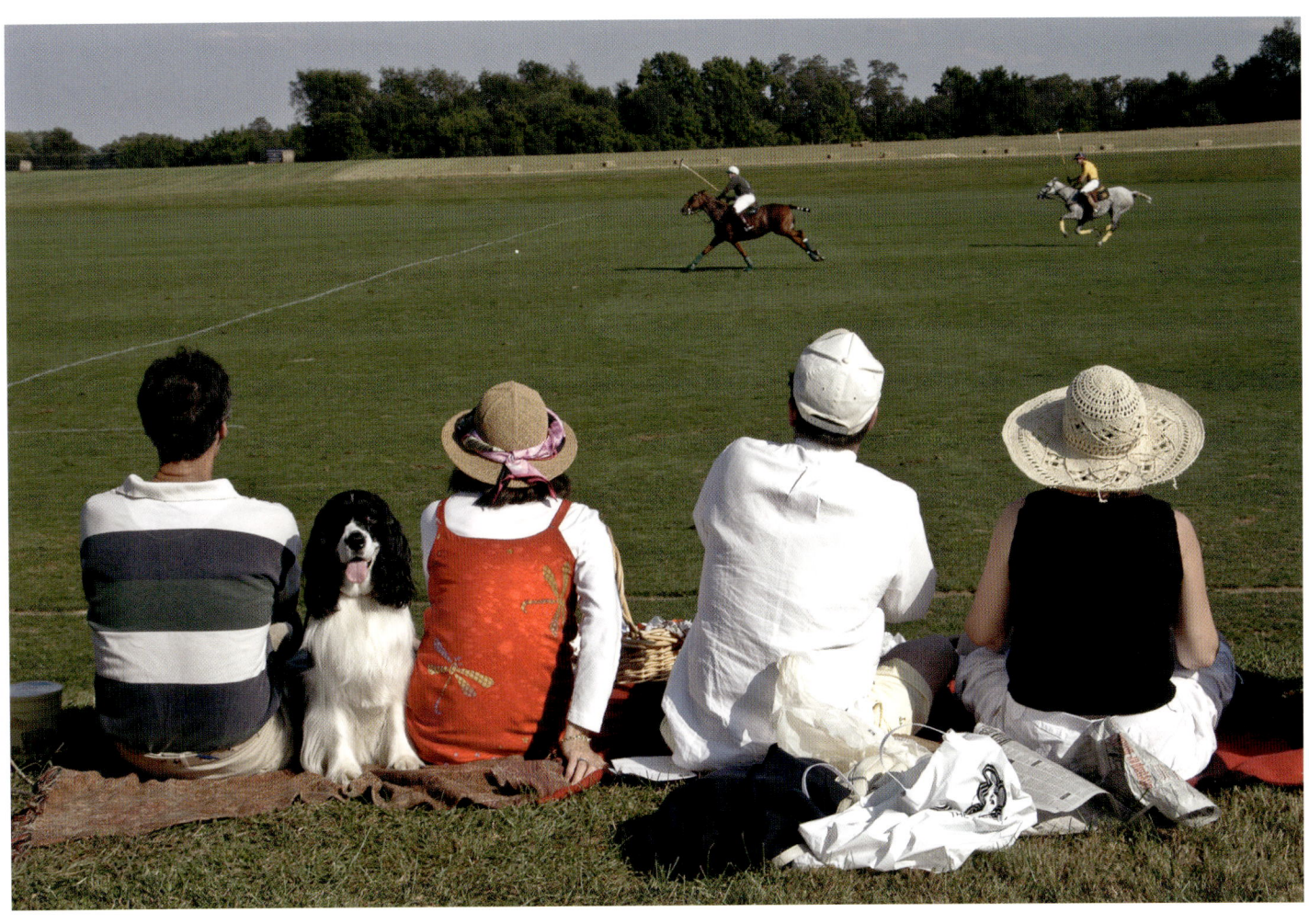

West Marlboro Township
Plantation Field, popular for Three Day Eventing, horse racing, Tough Mudder competitions, and other activities

West Marlboro Township
Kick ball

New Garden Township
Brandywine Polo Club

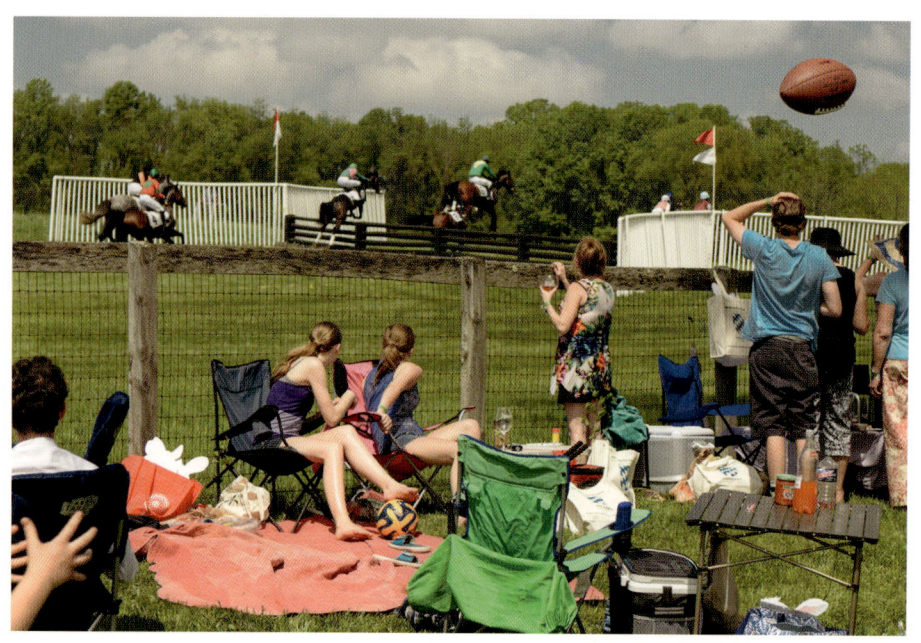
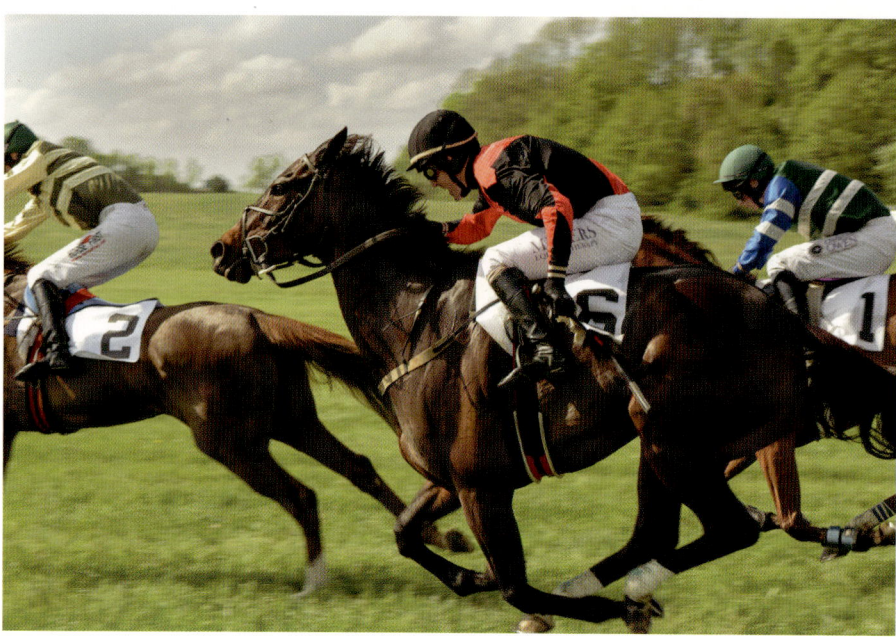

East Marlboro Township
Willowdale Steeplechase

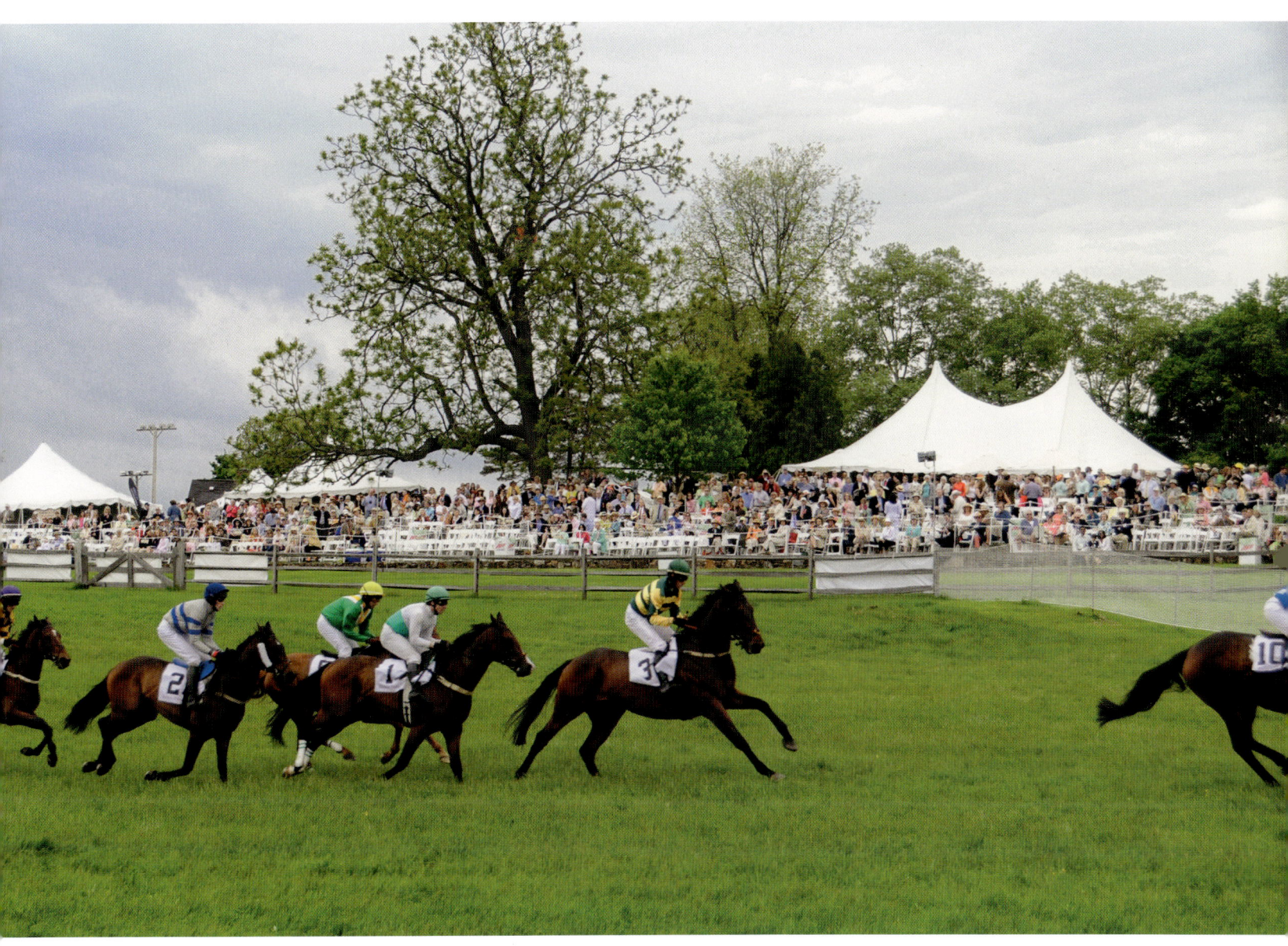

Willistown Township
Radnor Races for Brandywine Conservancy

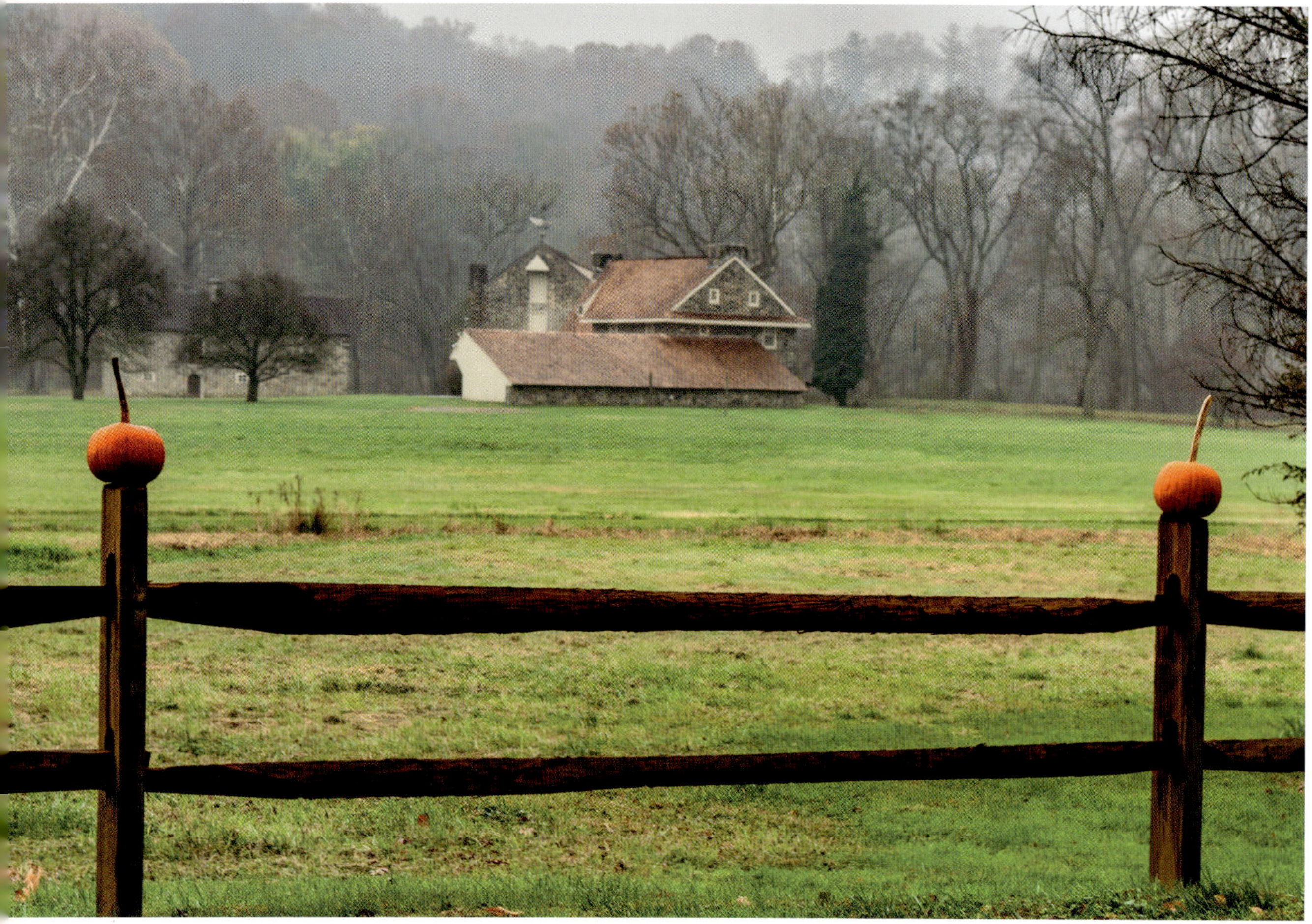

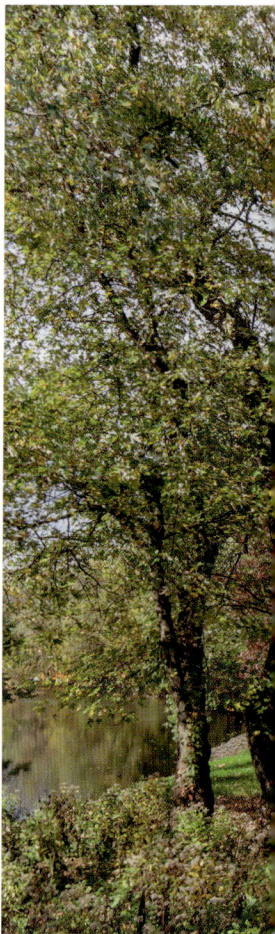

Birmingham Township
Historic farm along Brandywine Creek

Birmingham Township
Brandywine River Museum of Art

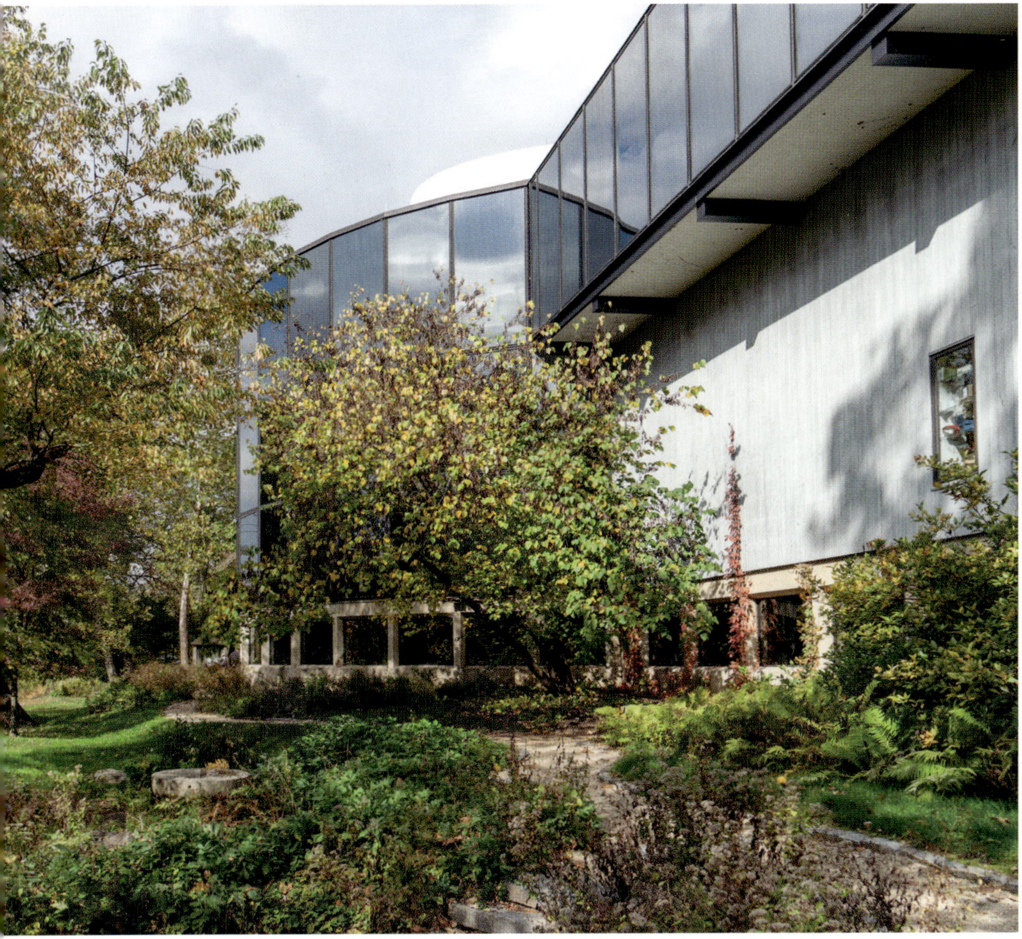

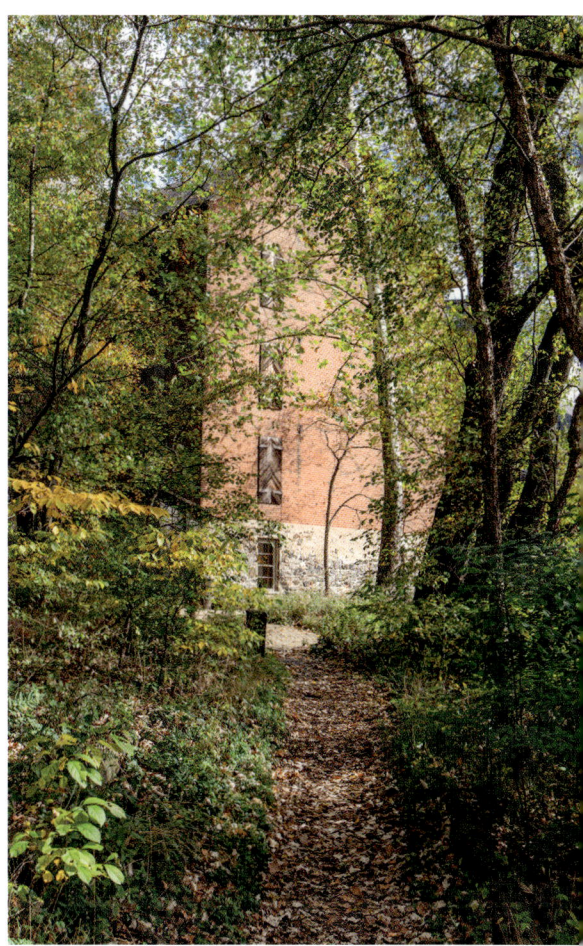

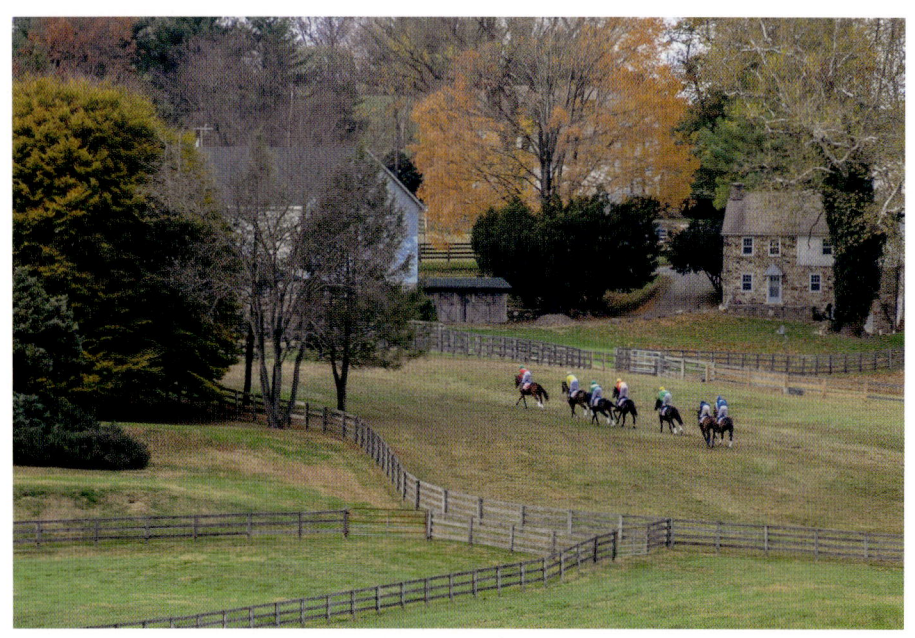

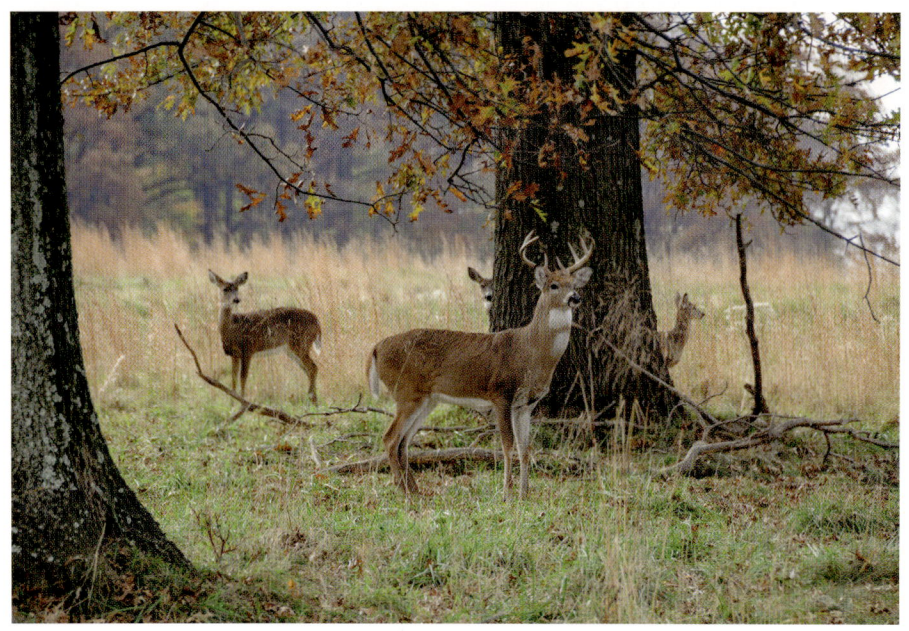

West Marlborough Township
Pennsylvania Hunt Cup

Local wildlife

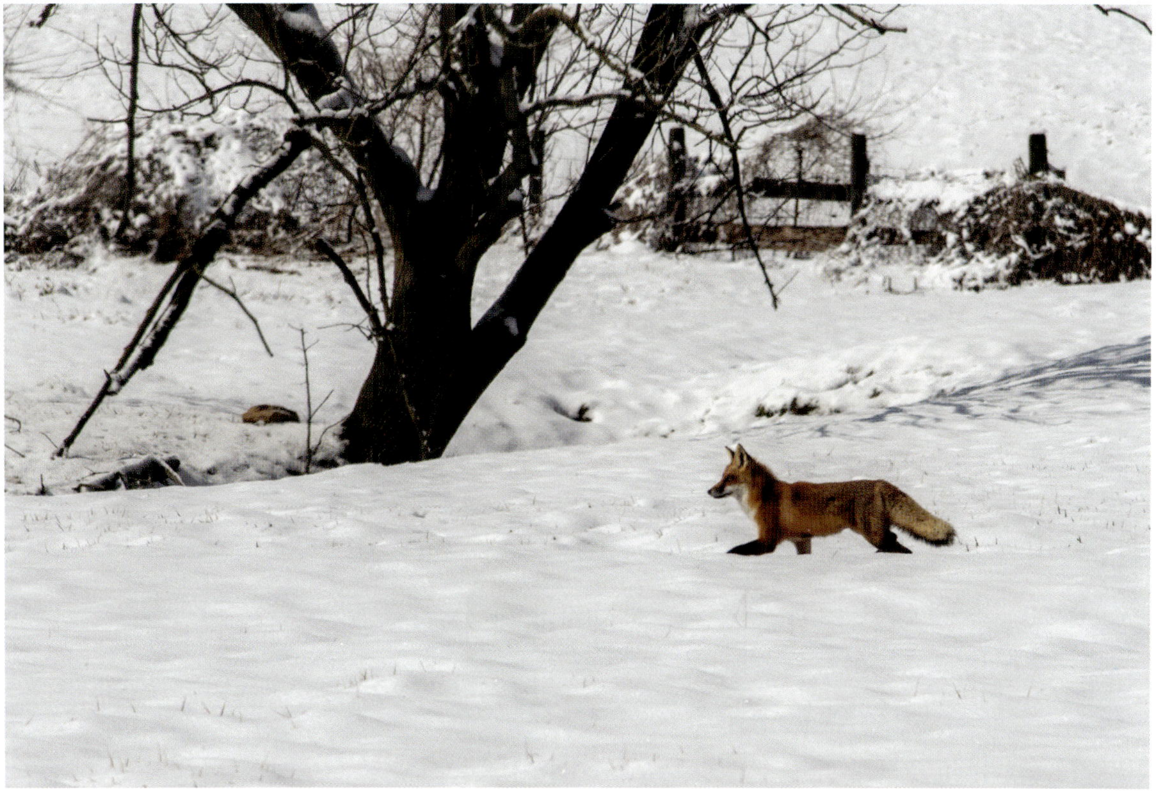

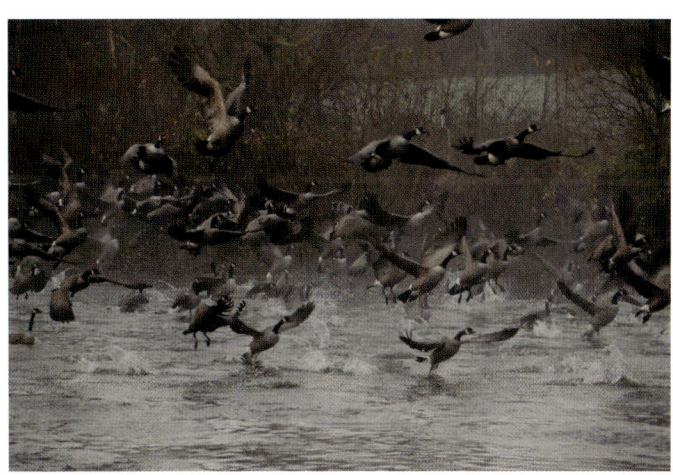
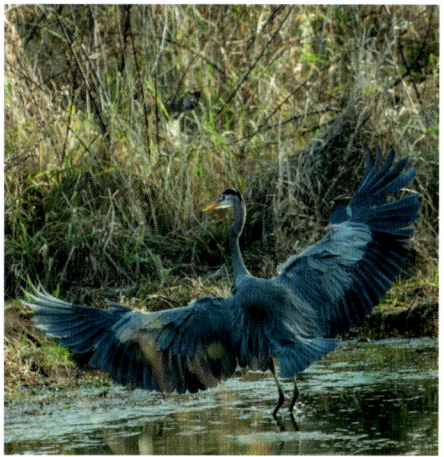

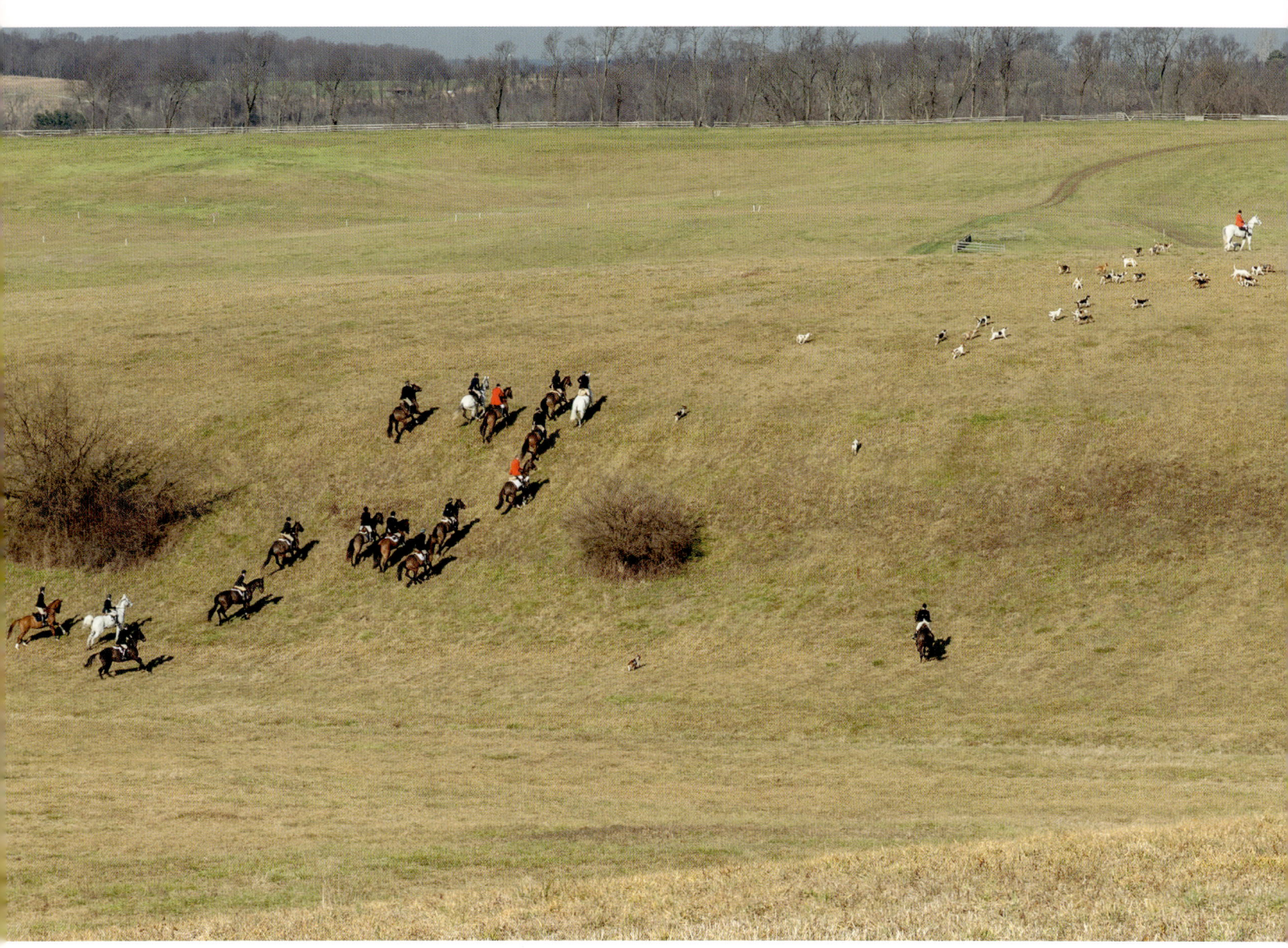

East Marlborough Township
Fox hunting with Cheshire hounds,
Thanksgiving Meet

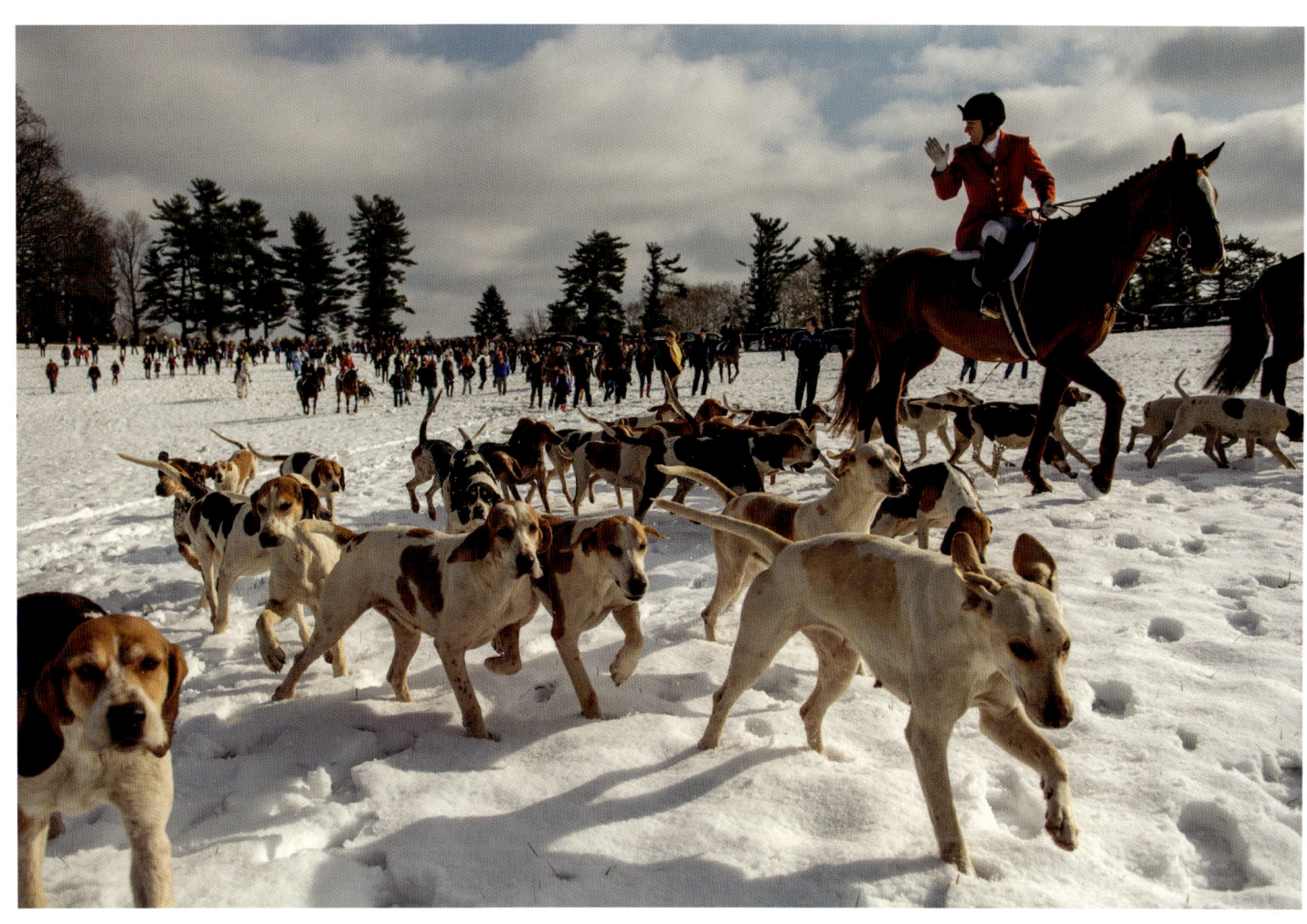

East Marlborough Township
Fox hunting

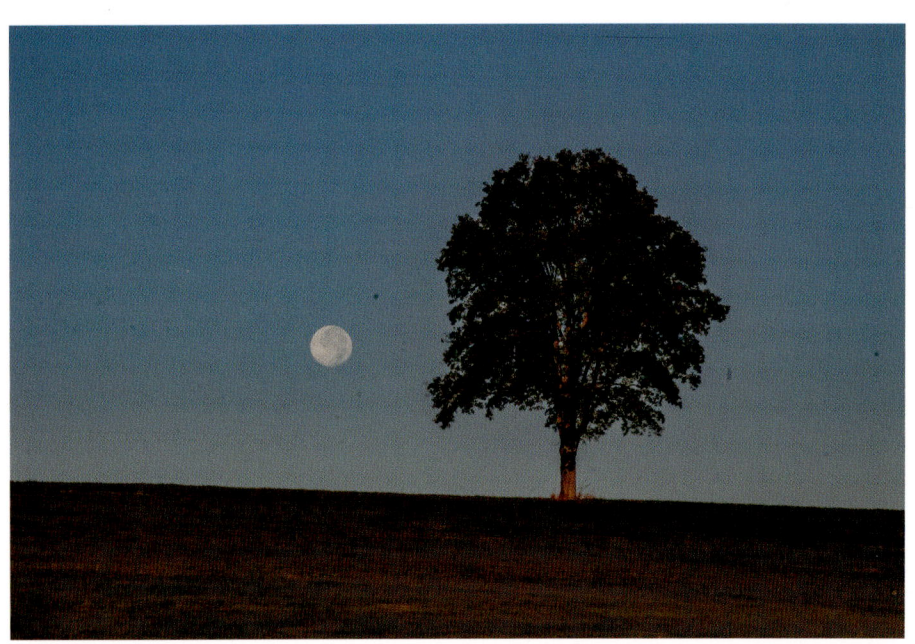

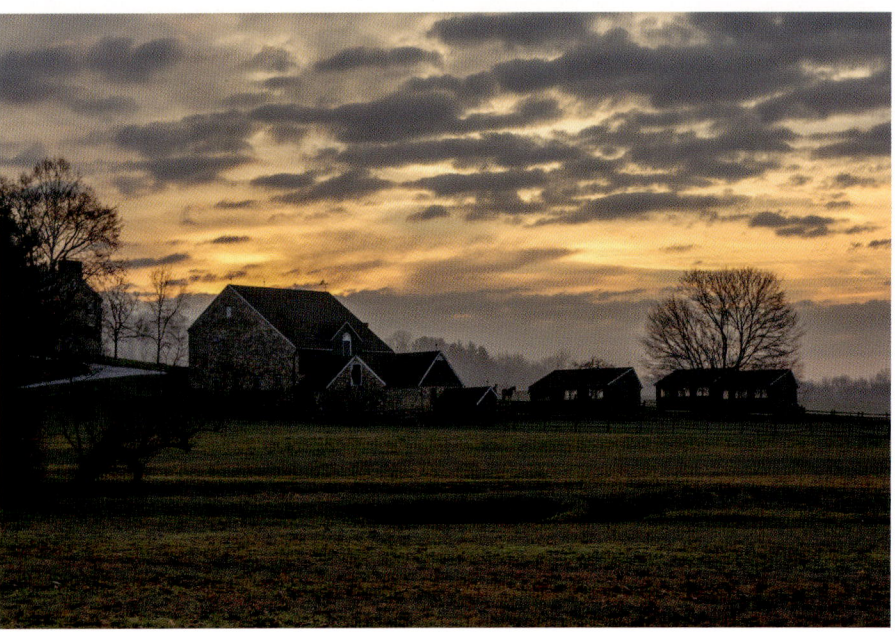

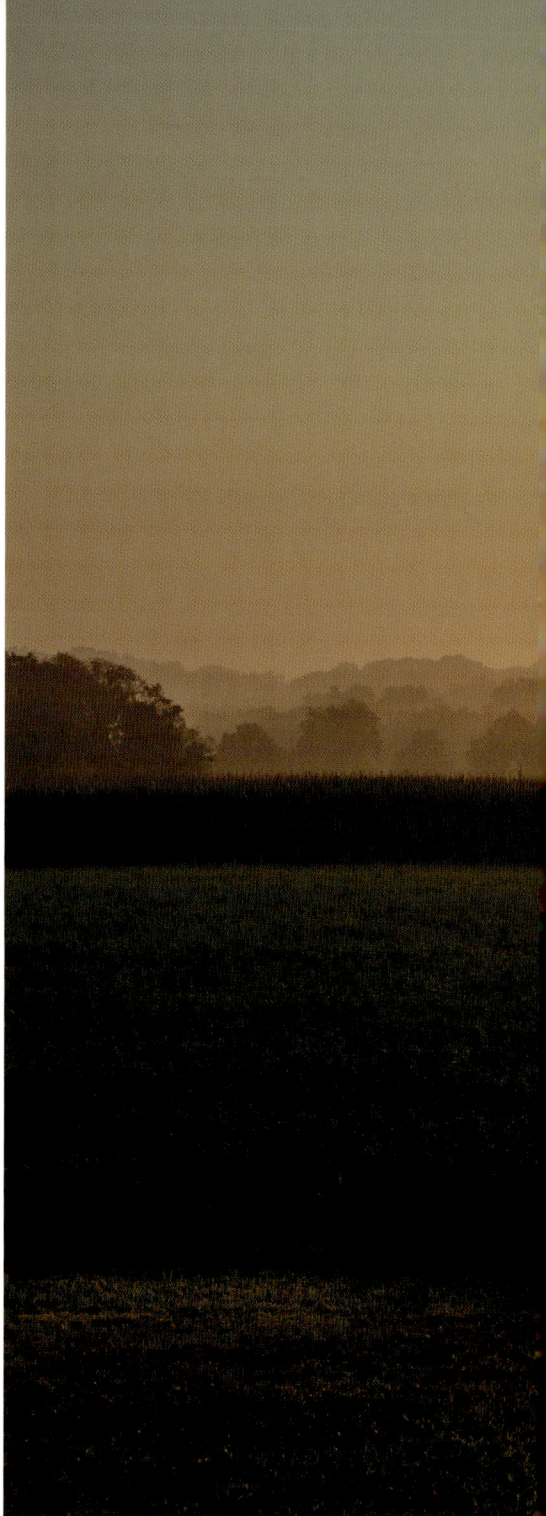

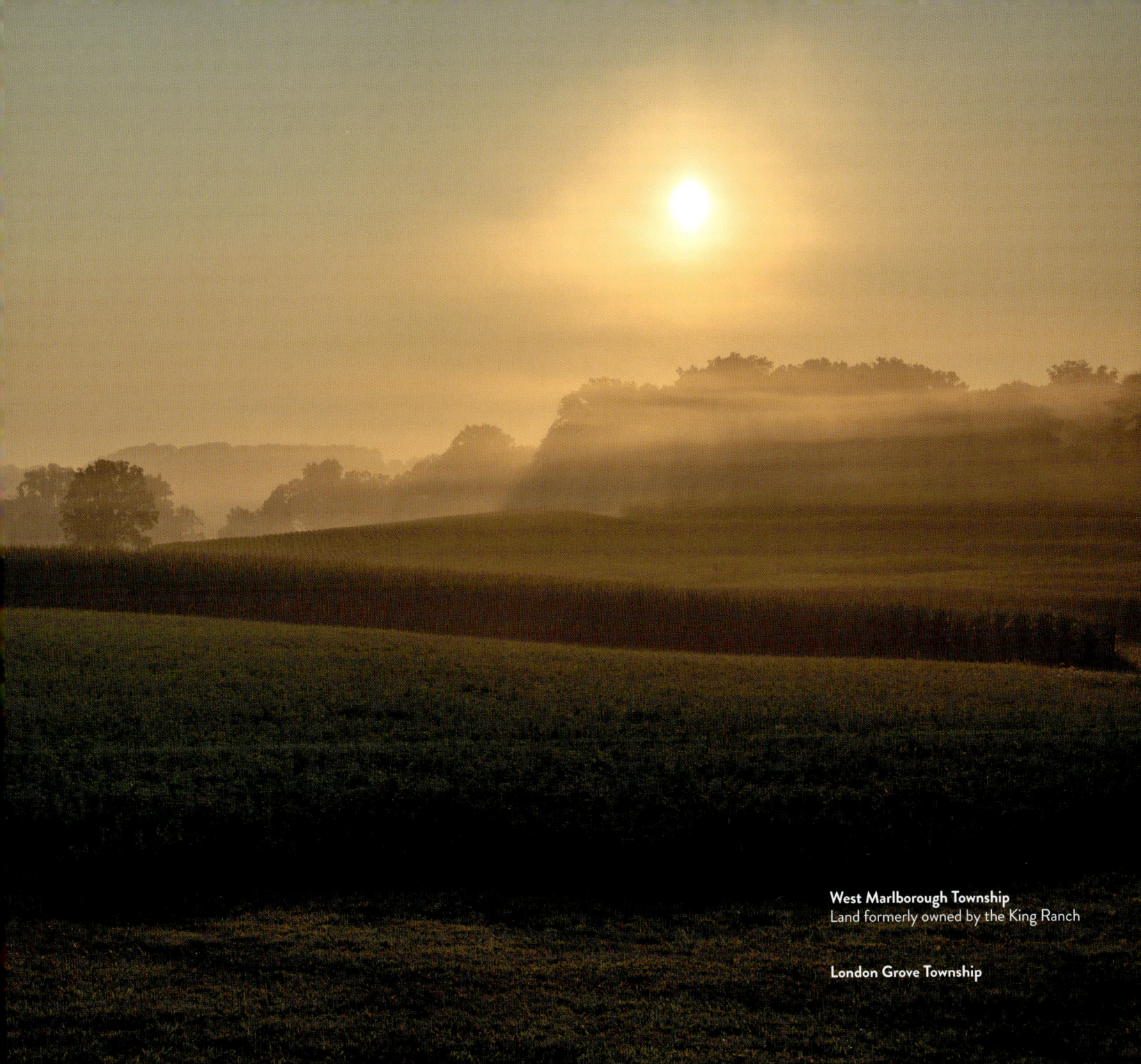

West Marlborough Township
Land formerly owned by the King Ranch

London Grove Township

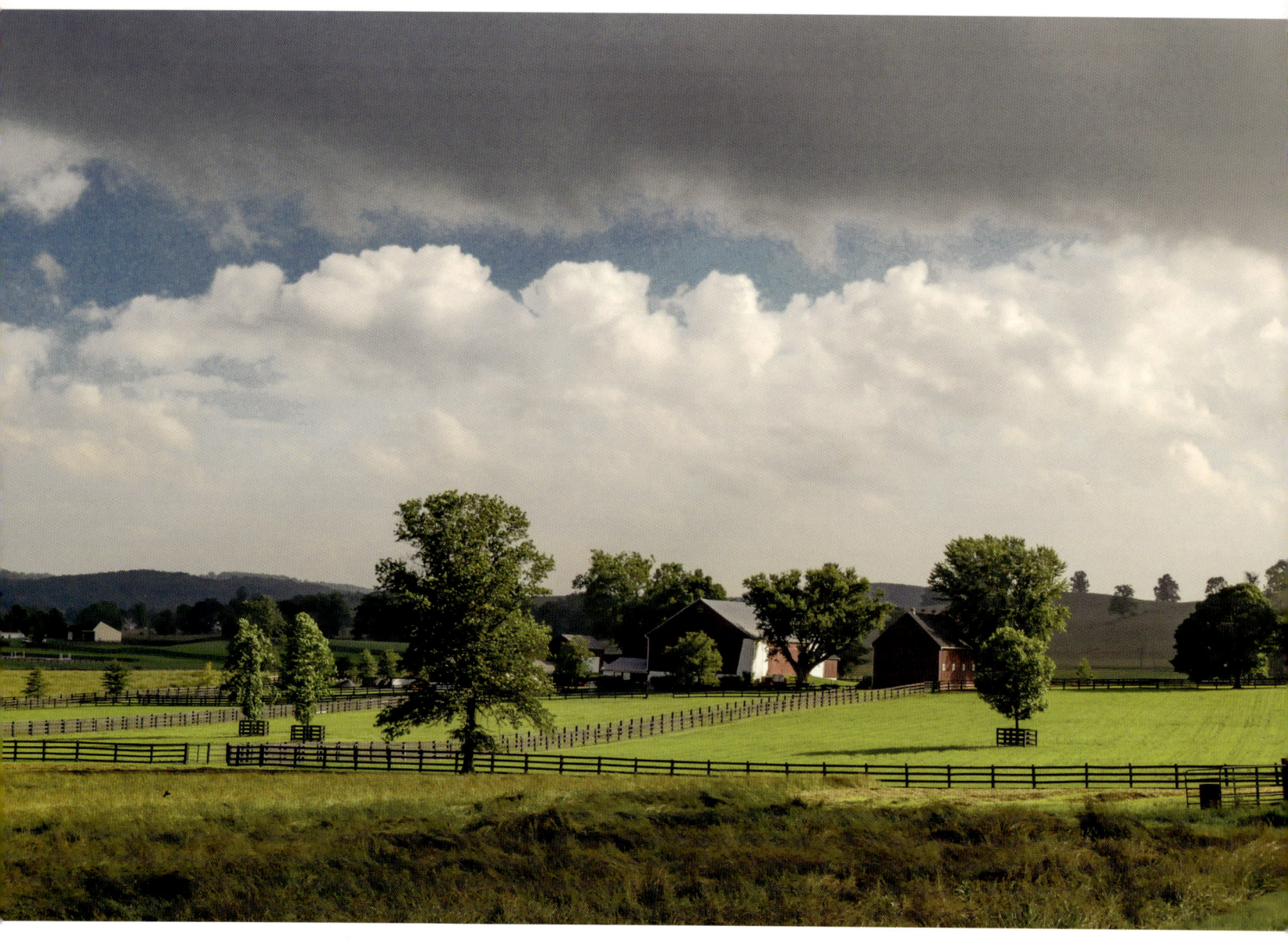
West Marlborough Township

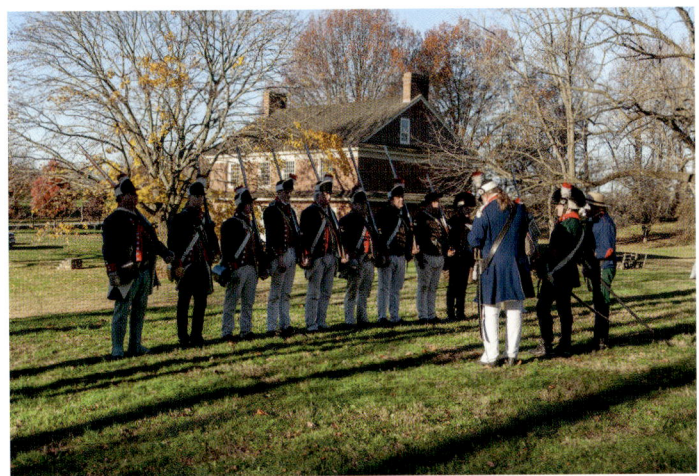
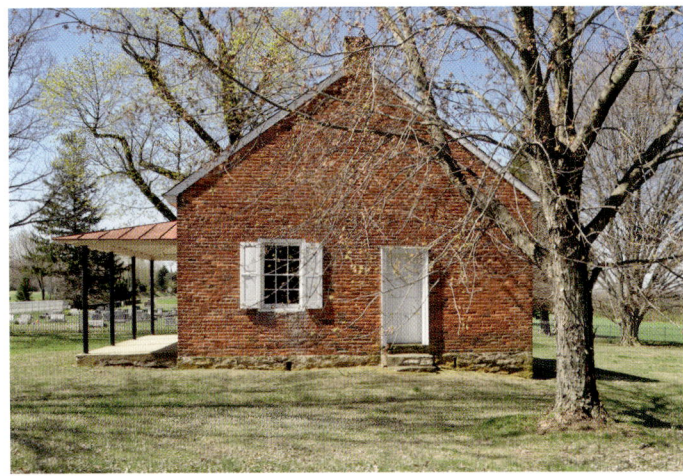
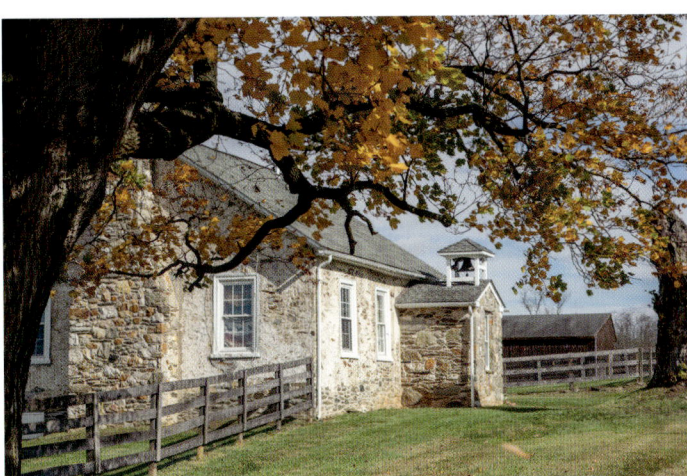
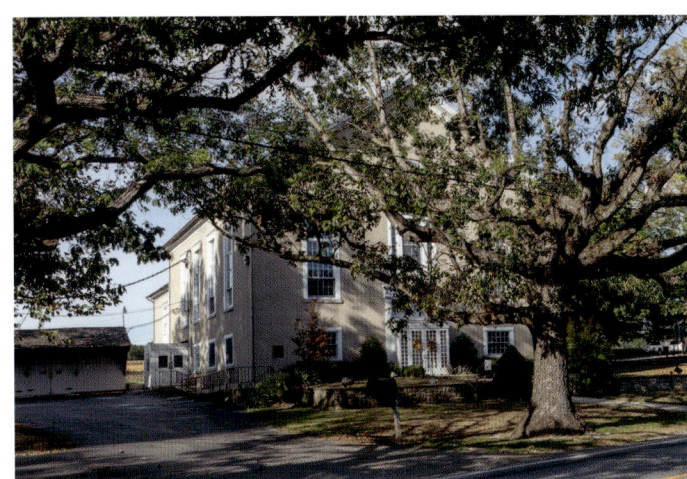

Primitive Hall, West Marlboro Township
The 4th Continental Light Dragoons encamp by the substantial house built in 1738 by Joseph Pennock.

West Marlborough Township
Old school house

Upper Oxford Township
Homeville Meeting House

Londonderry Township
Manor Presbyterian Church, Fagg's Manor

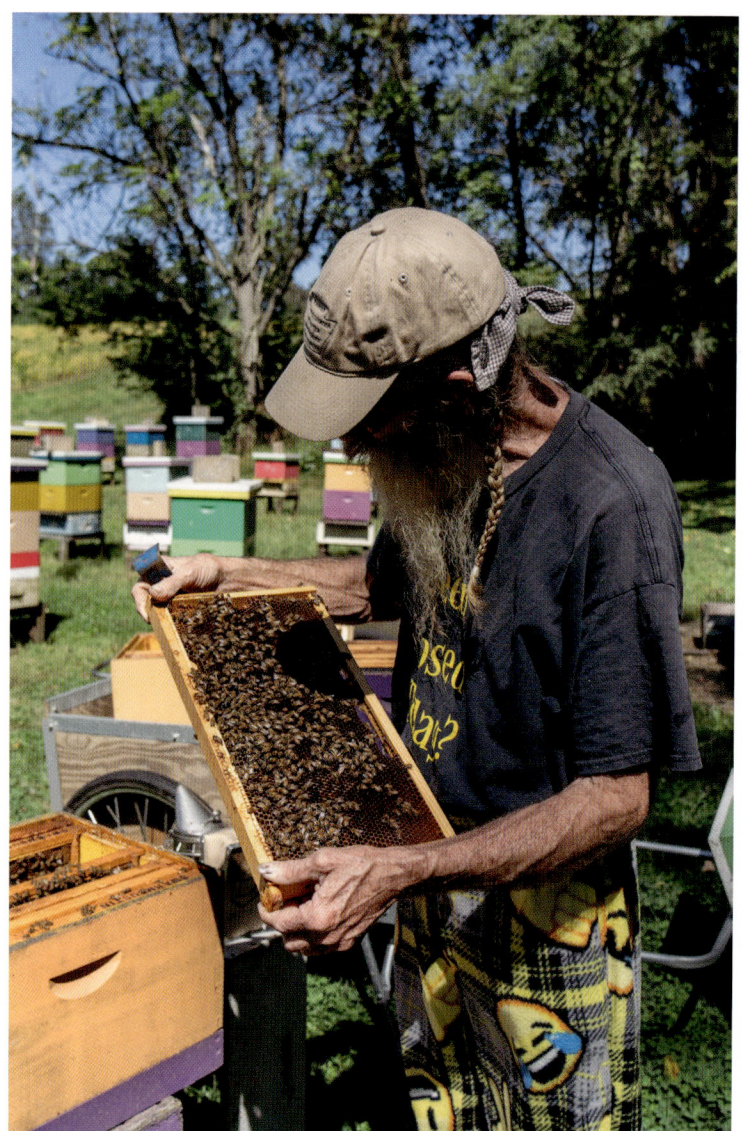
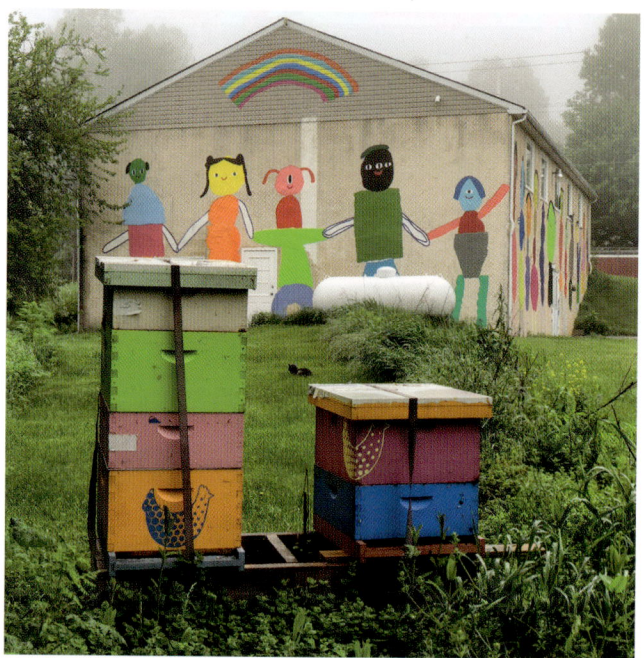
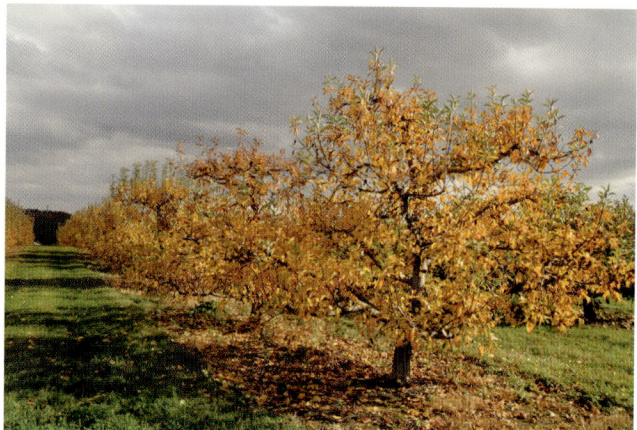

West Marlborough Township
Bee keeping

Londonderry Township
Street Road Artists' Space is a small, unique gallery devoted to shows that pertain to land and place.

London Grove Township

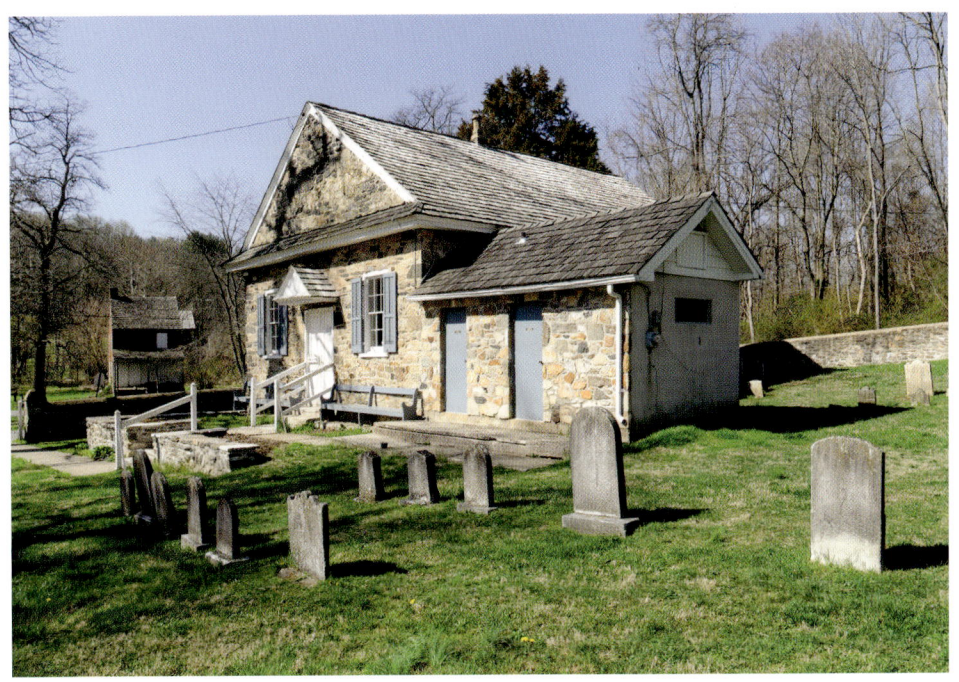
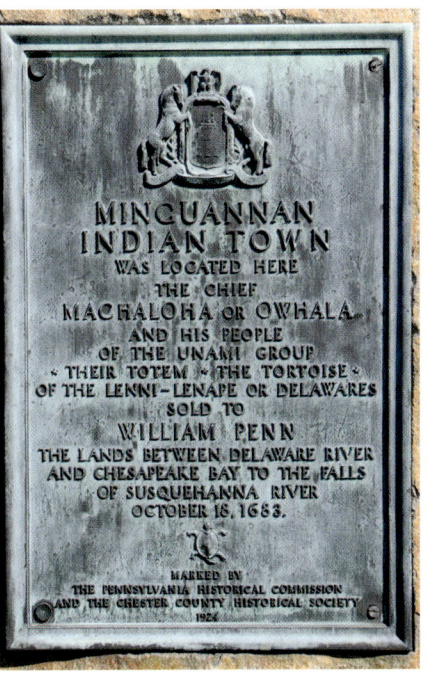

London Tract Meeting House, London Britain Township
A memorial tablet reads: "Minguannan Indian Town was located here. The chief, Machaloha or Owhala, and his people of the Unami Group—their totem, the tortoise of the Lenni-Lenape or Delaware—sold to William Penn the land between Delaware River and Chesapeake Bay to the falls of Susquehanna River, October 18, 1683."

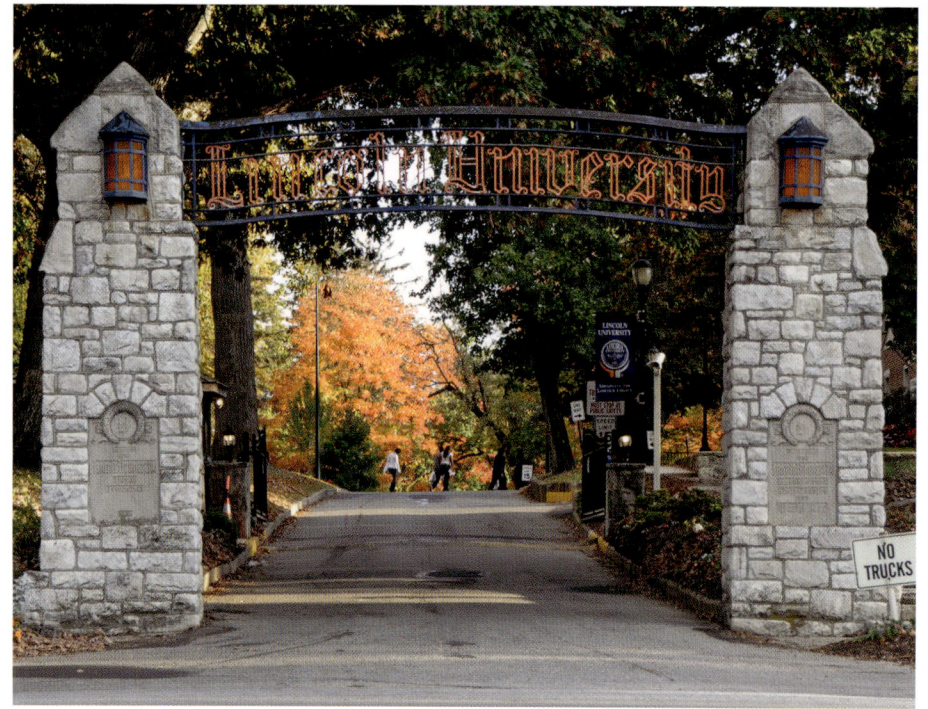
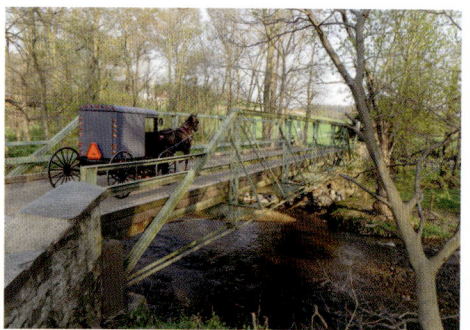
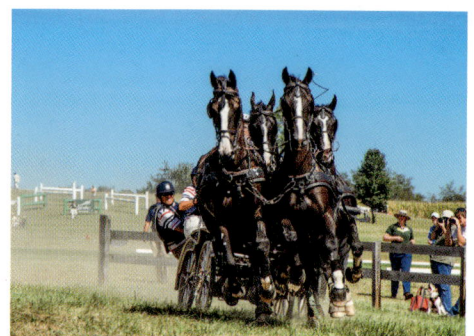

Lincoln University, Lower Oxford Township

West Nottingham Township
Octoraro River, the western boundary of Chester County

London Grove Township

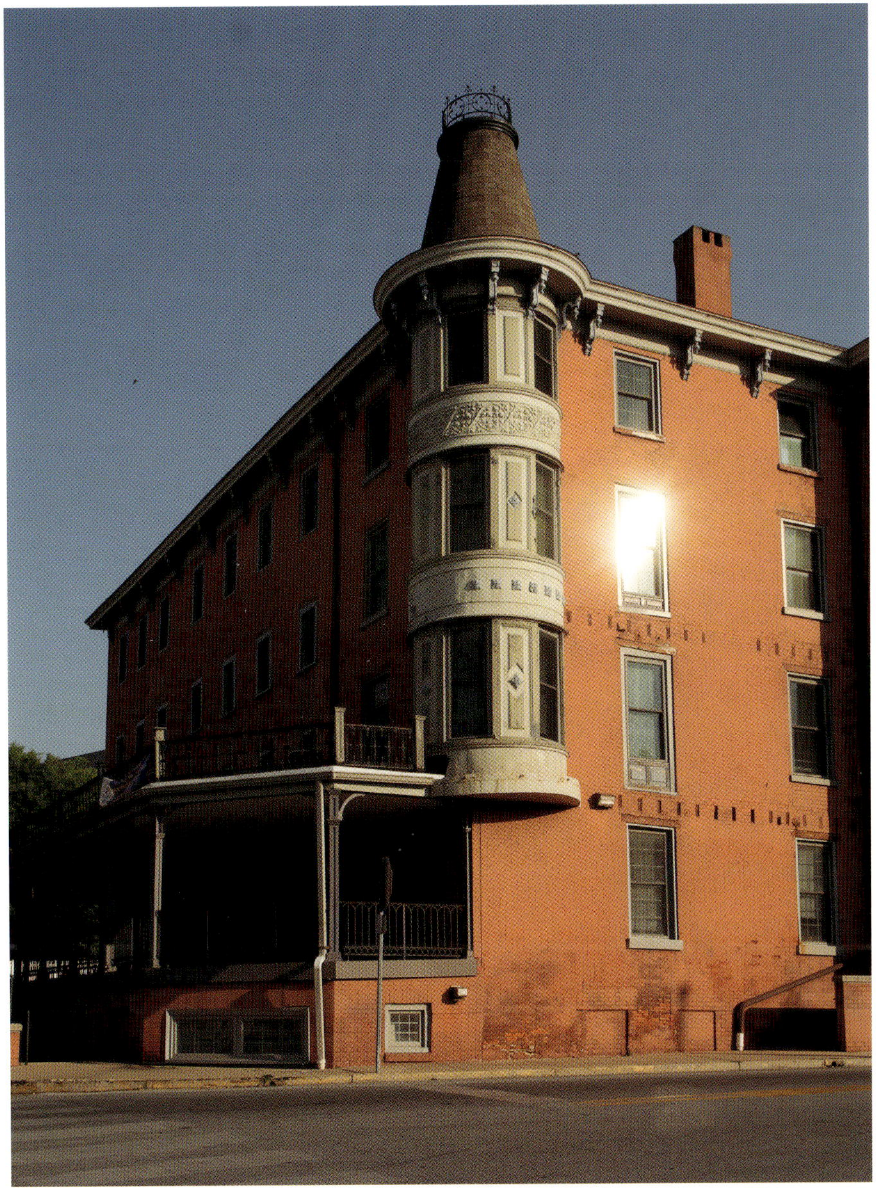

Oxford

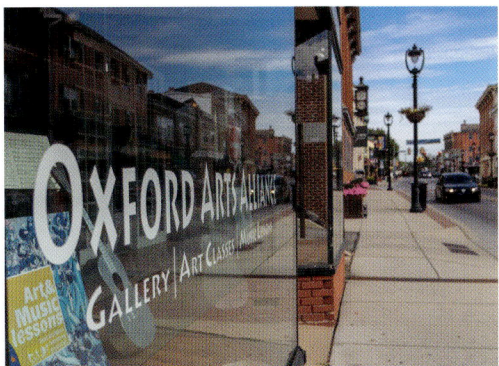
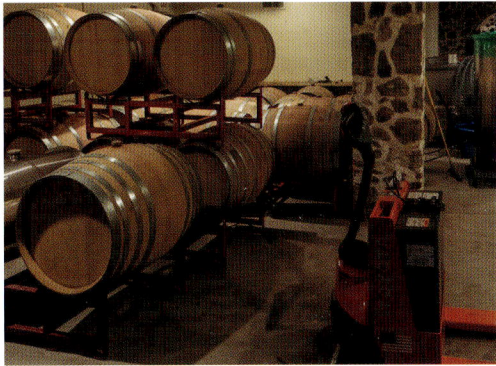
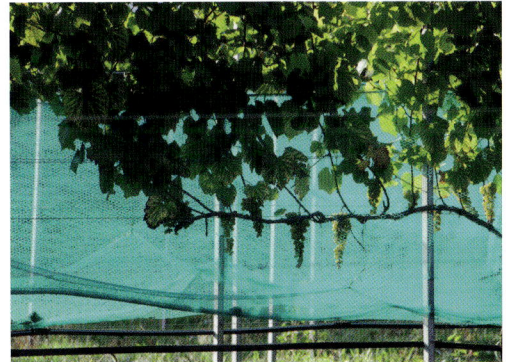

A number of tasty wines are produced in Chester County.

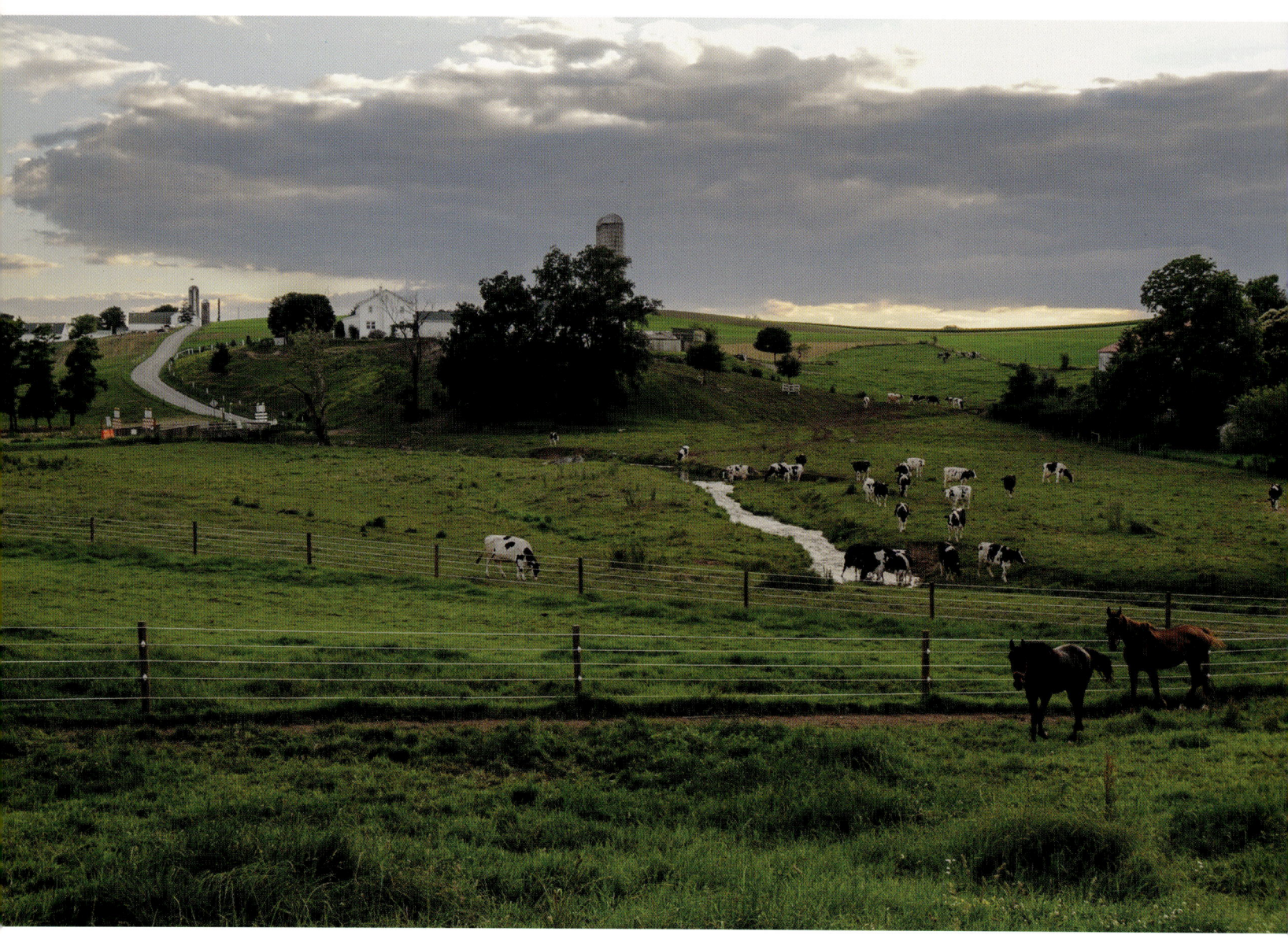

Lower Oxford Township

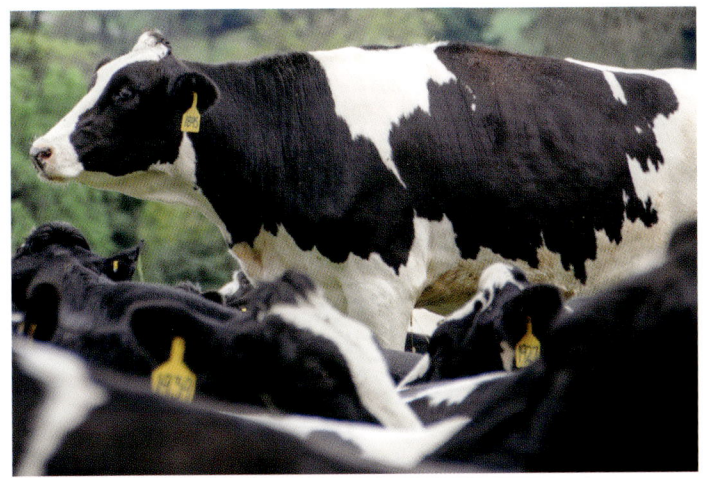
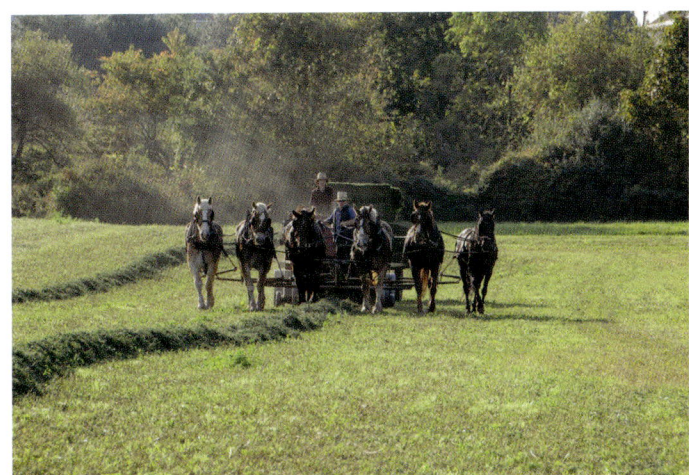
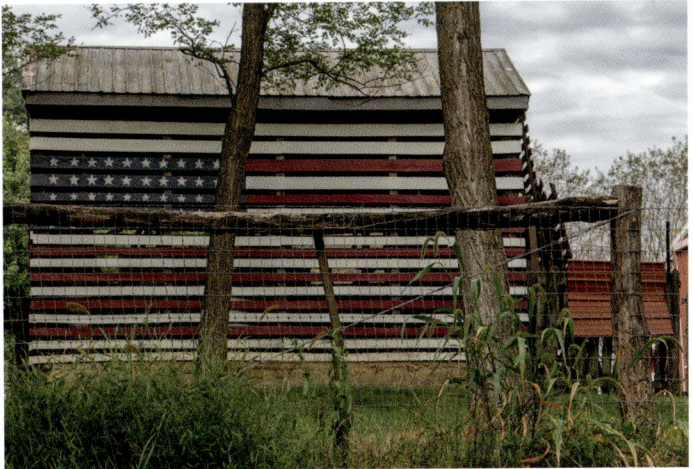
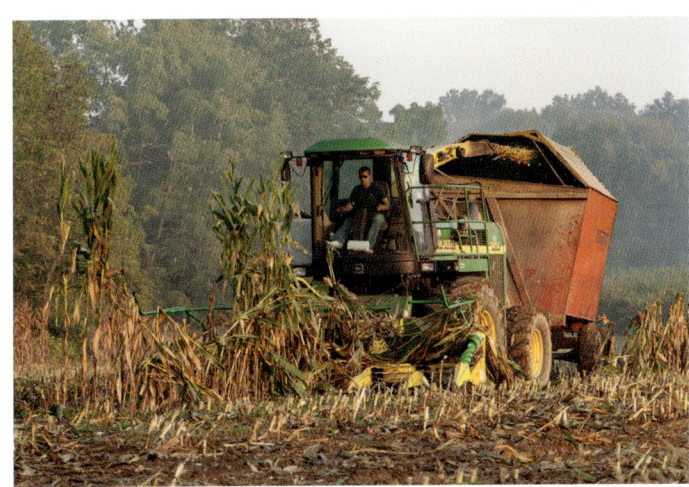

Holstein cows support the county's robust dairy production.

West Nottingham Township

East Nottingham Township

West Nottingham Township

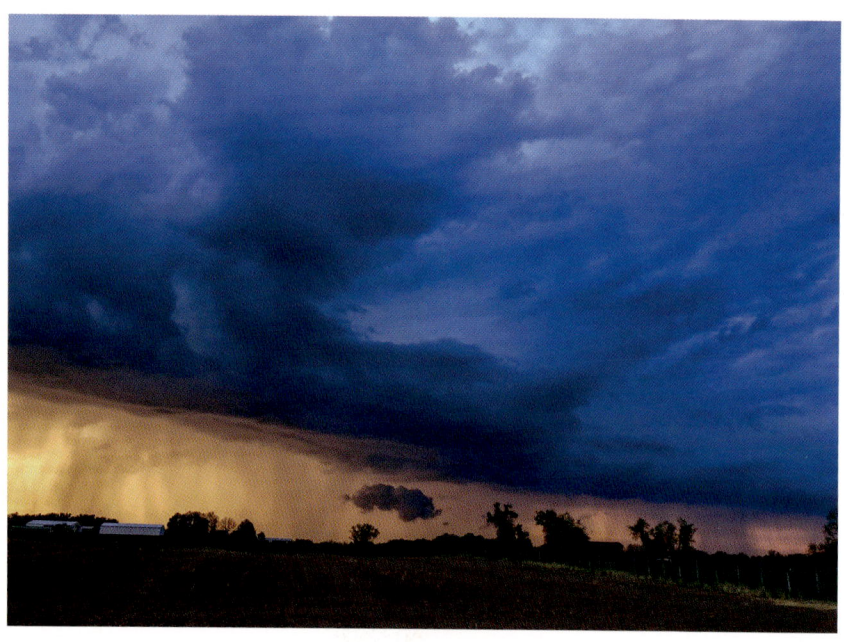

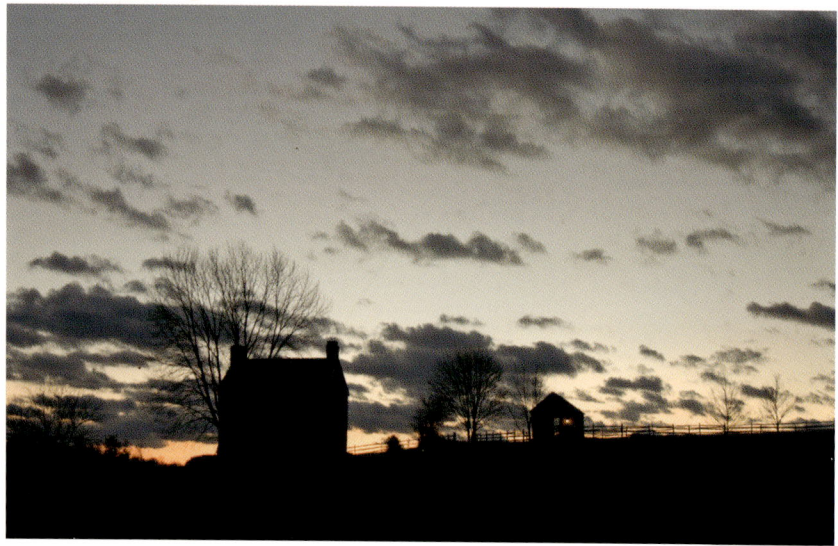

London Grove Township

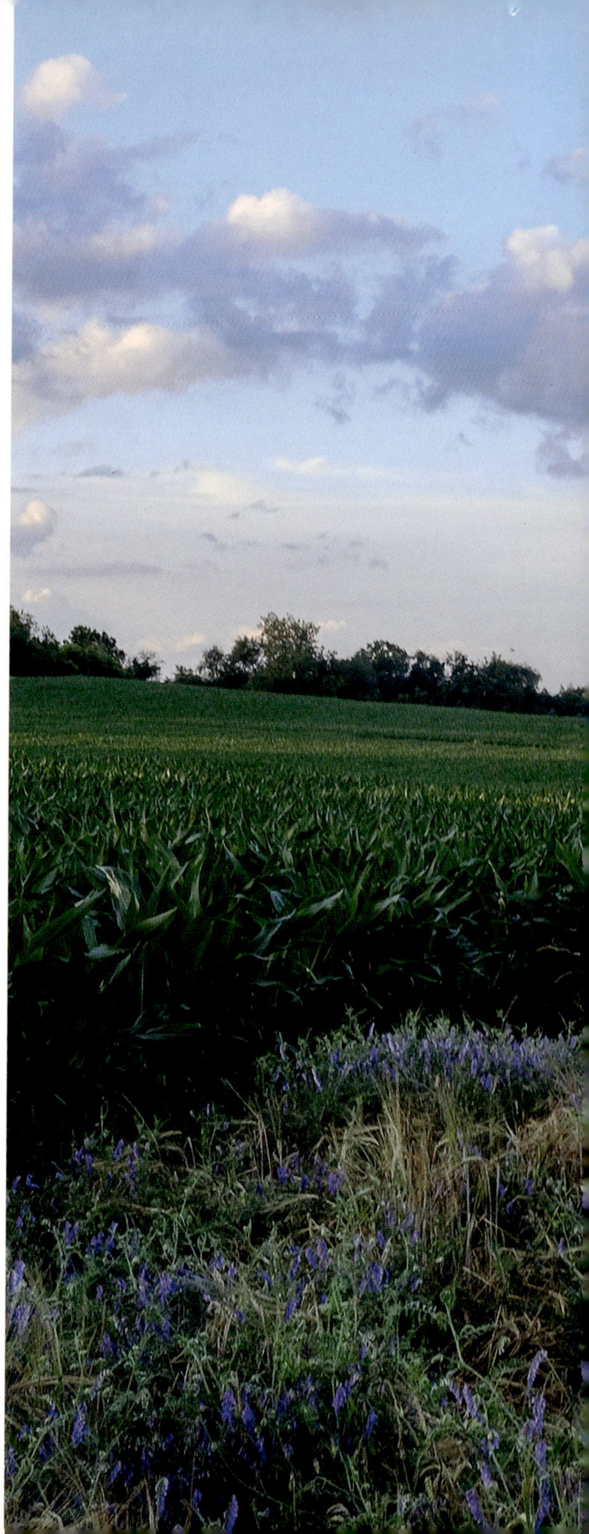

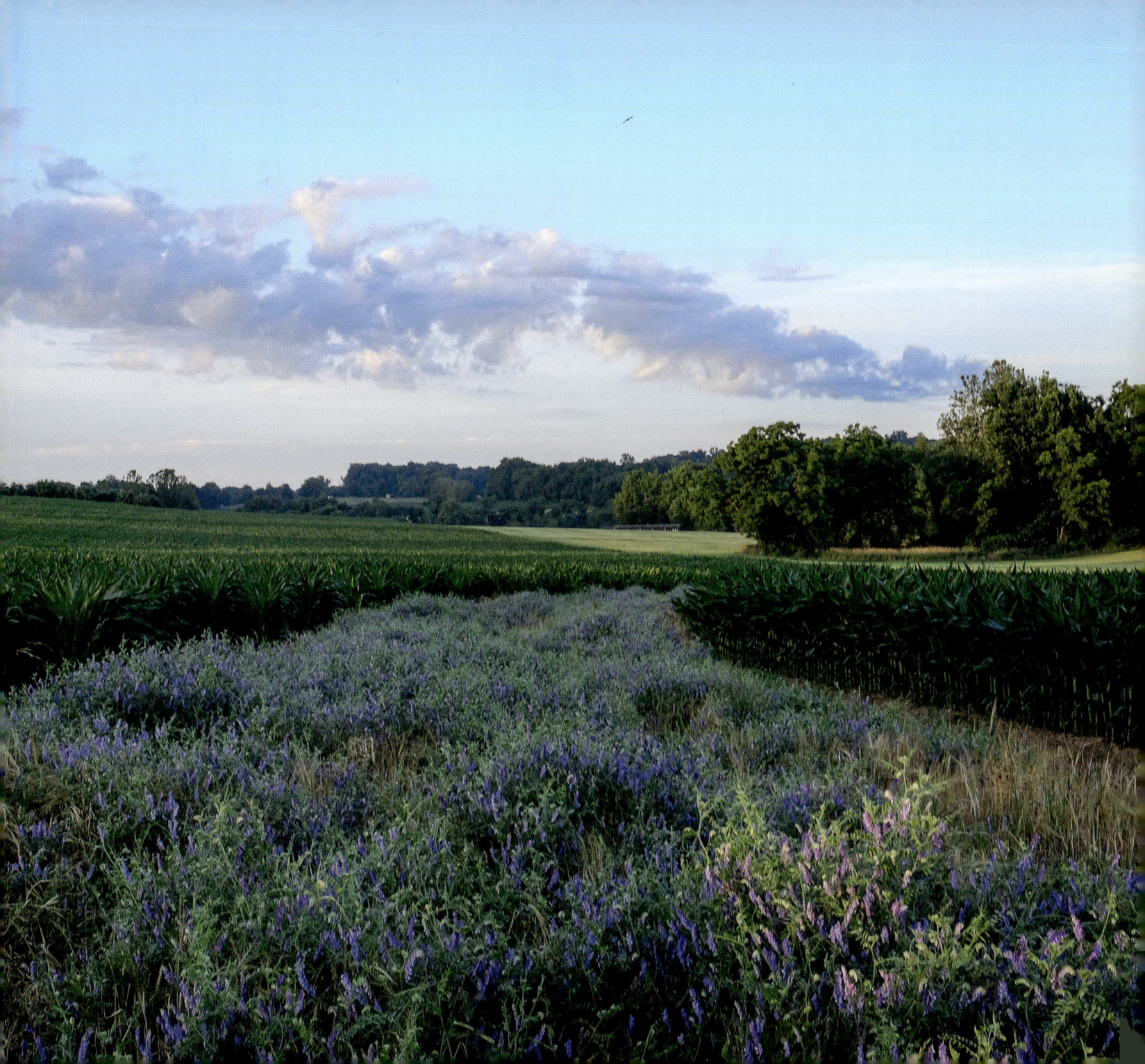

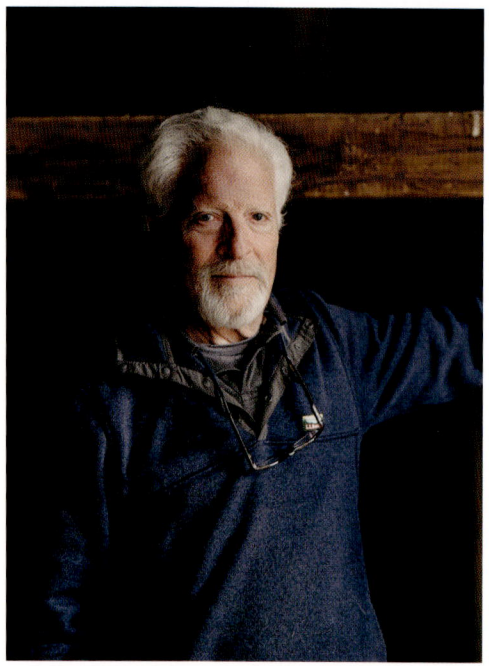

Antelo Devereux Jr. has been taking photographs since he was given a Kodak Duaflex II box camera at age ten. He is a graduate of Harvard University and has taken courses at the Maine Media Center. He has exhibited in Maine, Vermont, Pennsylvania, and Delaware and has published ten books of his images. He spends his time in Pennsylvania and Maine.